Richard Stephens has been in practice for some forty years, working primarily in the technology sector. He has seen the law from the angle of both a litigator and a non-contentious lawyer and brings to bear his experience in both of these fields. Richard first qualified as a barrister before moving in-house to work at two prominent IT companies in the 90's and then requalifying as a solicitor to become a partner in two City of London Law firms. He set up his own practice in 2004 and since then has worked as mediator and arbitrator in numerous cases as well as establishing himself as a trainer in the area of commercial legal subjects, including a half-day session looking specifically at contractual indemnities. He is a Fellow of the Chartered Institute of Arbitrators, of the British Computer Society and of the Society for Computers & Law (of which he is a past Chair).

Stephens on Contractual Indemnities

Stephens on Contractual Indemnities

Richard Stephens FCIArb, FBCS,
Fellow of the Society for Computers & Law

Law Brief Publishing

Published 2021 by Law Brief Publishing, an imprint of Law Brief Publishing Ltd
30 The Parks
Minehead
Somerset
TA24 8BT

www.lawbriefpublishing.com

Paperback: 978-1-912687-91-6

PREFACE

This book is about "contractual" indemnities – it concerns the use of an indemnity in a commercial (non-consumer) contract. Sometimes this is referred to as a "contract of indemnity", though an indemnity may just be one clause of many in a regular commercial contract. Of course, many insurance contracts are contracts of indemnity, but this book is not about such contracts, though some reference to insurance law is inevitable at points. While by no means a modern creation, the contractual indemnity has recently blossomed to become a much loved drafting tool and modern business contracts are replete with indemnities covering a wide variety of situations.

This book aims to demystify the contractual indemnity by looking at how the courts today typically treat indemnity clauses. This book will have to look at the disparate cases on the subject and try to draw lessons from them – not easy when there is little in the way of underlying guiding principle. It will be necessary to look at many cases, recite their facts and state their conclusions. This little book then seeks to set out the conclusions in something like a coherent statement of a new "law of contractual indemnities" along with the practice points that can be gleaned from the cases. For that reason, this book gives the indemnities discussed in the cases in full, rather than paraphrasing them, as much often depends on the very words used.

While cases on indemnities go back hundreds of years, this book focuses on modern case-law, although some modern cases have on occasion had to look at much older ones, not always to follow them, and sometimes to point up their inconsistencies. Indeed, there is a noticeable trend in modern cases on indemnities to depart from nineteenth century approaches in favour of the modern law's more straightforward approach to the construction of contracts.

Indeed, older indemnity cases should be treated with caution: many depend on the application of contra proferentem as an aid to construction, which is decidedly out of judicial favour now, or the application of the Canada Steamship guidelines, which have a somewhat dubious status in the modern law, as will shortly be seen. Furthermore, very early cases on indemnities were influenced by the division of English Law into common law and equity: the common law could only award damages, while equity could not award damages but could order specific performance of an indemnity. To award damages, the common law needed to find actual loss which arguably required payment by the indemnified prior to recovering under an indemnity. This distinction was lost with the fusion of law and equity in the 1870's, but the cases decided before then, and those decided subsequently which still relied on the old distinction, have to some extent cast their shadow over the modern law. By and large, the searching light of the modern law is beginning to dispel the gloom cast by those shadows. However, as will be seen in these pages, even today, this distinction between common law and equity is still lively and capable of generating disputes around some aspects of contractual indemnities.

Equally, while there are many judgments out there on indemnities, given the restrictions on the length of this work, aimed as it is at practising lawyers, this book takes the line of only discussing those cases that are in the writer's opinion illustrative of an instructive point and not those – interesting as they are – which only serve to point up academic or historic controversies. There is indeed more to be said about contractual indemnities than this book has space to cover, but it is hoped that the practising lawyer will find much in these pages to dispel at least some of the misconceptions that have grown up around them.

Cases on contractual indemnities are appearing with increasing frequency reflecting their increased use in commercial contracts: the law in this book is stated to the best of the writer's knowledge as at 30 September 2020.

Richard Stephens
October 2020

CONTENTS

CHAPTER ONE
WHAT IS AN INDEMNITY?

"... In English law an indemnity is a promise to prevent the indemnified person from suffering loss (damnum): see e.g. Firma C-Trade SA v Newcastle Protection and Indemnity Association (The "Fanti" and "The Padre Island") [1991] 2 AC 1, 35 (Lord Goff). ..."[1]

The subtitle of this Chapter could usefully be, "what is <u>not</u> an indemnity?"

Introduction

There used to be but one indemnity in most commercial agreements and it was the IPR (intellectual property rights) indemnity. It provides, in a sense, protection for both parties and is a good example of an indemnity. It is a commonplace in e.g. software licences and many other types of agreement. For the licensee, it provides peace of mind, an assurance that, if a third party should emerge to claim rights in the IPR which have been licensed to that licensee, then the licensor will be responsible for that claim. For the licensor, it also provides peace of mind: if the licensor is licensing its own IPR, it wants to make sure that it is the one dealing with allegations of infringement, not anyone else. Indeed, the licensor

---

[1] *per* Leggatt LJ in *Minera Las Bambas v Glencore* [2019] EWCA Civ 972

may well be in the best place to defend any such allegation of infringement. It is perhaps a rare example of where an indemnity has benefits for both parties and is a sensible allocation of risk, as was observed by Arnold J in *Codemasters v Automobile Club de l'Ouest* [2009] EWHC 2361 (Ch):

> "*Not only is such an indemnity commonplace, but also there are good reasons why parties agree to such indemnities. Generally speaking, the licensor of intellectual property rights will be in a better position to assess whether the exploitation will infringe third party intellectual property rights. This is particularly true in the field of copyright. To a lesser extent, it is true of trade marks also. Furthermore, in terms of allocation of risk, generally speaking it will be commercially more acceptable for the risk of a claim of infringement by a third party to be borne by the licensor than by the licensee.*"

Of course, whether an individual IPR indemnity actually achieves those aims will depend on the precise drafting: it is the aim of this book to look at indemnities and how the courts apply them so as to be able to answer that question.

While there is some reference in these pages to the treatment of an indemnity in the world of insurance, this is kept to a minimum as insurance law responds to different challenges. For example, contractual indemnities do not require any duty of disclosure by the indemnified to the indemnifier, unlike the duty of disclosure owed by an insured to the insurer. Furthermore, insurance is often about extreme events that are not realistically contemplated as likely to happen (such as a disastrous fire burning down a factory) whereas a contractual indemnity may be for an event that is very much on the indemnified's mind (such as an indemnity against losses caused by the indemnifier's breach of contract). So, while they are similar, they are by no means identical, and the focus of this book is on those indemnities that appear in ordinary commercial contracts between businesses.

The other question addressed by this book is whether an indemnity in other commercial contexts has the same hallmarks of being a sensible allocation of risk as with the IPR indemnity. This is because, in recent years, the contractual indemnity has become a much loved tool of the commercial lawyer and has gone way beyond the IPR indemnity. Indemnity provisions are more or less ubiquitous now and appear scattered throughout most modern commercial contracts. Whether they survive the drafting into the final signed version is a different question as indemnities have attracted an aura of fear among lawyers asked to review contracts. Having said which, if those insisting on including indemnities in commercial contracts knew just how devoid of underlying principle they were, it might start some debate about the value of including them in the first place.

Terminology

As indemnities have become common in commercial contracts, so certain language, certain formulae, have also become common in commercial contracts. Indeed, some expressions have become "hallowed" by usage, such that it seems inconceivable that an indemnity should not contain them e.g.

"Defend and hold harmless"

"Save and hold harmless"

"Indemnify and keep indemnified"

Indeed, we see combinations of these expressions using elements drawn from each of them, such as "defend, save and hold harmless" and sometimes a clause will use all of these elements in one long, inelegant expression.

However, research in most legal dictionaries and textbooks to do with contract or commercial law will not yield any clue as to the meaning of such expressions. Let us therefore look at the formula "hold harmless": it is very common and will be seen in just about any indemnity provision, but what exactly does it mean?

A Canadian case throws some light on this question. In *Salmon River Logging v Burt Bros.* [1953] 2 SCR 117, Burt Bros. supplied trucks and personnel to operate them in Salmon River's logging yard. One of the trucks was standing idle by a spar tree (a tree used as a sort of crane). A workman working for Salmon River was yarding a log which caused the spar tree to collapse on the truck causing damage to it. Salmon River could not deny the negligent act but relied on clause 3 in the contract which provided that Burt Bros

> "... will indemnify and save harmless [Salmon River] from any claims or damage that may occur arising out of the use or operation of the said trucks for the term of the within contract."

The Supreme Court of Canada held that the clause did not cover negligence by Salmon River: the truck was standing idle at the time of the accident and the accident had nothing to do with the operation of the truck. Salmon River was therefore liable to Burt Bros for its negligence in damaging the truck[2]. Rand J said this,

> "We do not 'indemnify and save harmless' from or against our own claims ... [T]his familiar phrase must be given its well established meaning. To indemnify and save harmless is to protect one person against action in the nature of claims made or proceedings taken against him by a third person."

Before the reader leaps to the conclusion that "indemnify and save harmless" has this fixed judicial understanding, let us now look at what the UK Supreme Court made of very similar wording in *Farstad Supply v Enviroco (The Far Service)* [2010] UKSC 18[3]. In that case, the vessel "Far Service" was owned by Farstad and chartered to a third party, Asco. Asco had engaged Enviroco to clean out some of the Far Service's tanks. Following Asco's instructions, the master of the vessel started the engines just as an employee of Enviroco opened a valve which allowed oil to enter the engine room. The oil ignited due to the heat of the engine causing substantial damage. For the purposes of the action, it was assumed that Asco had been negligent.

Clause 33.5 of the charterparty provided that Farstad would

> "defend, indemnify and hold harmless [Asco] from and against any and all claims, demands, liabilities, proceedings and causes of action resulting from loss or damage in relation to the Vessel (including total loss) or property of the Owner ... irrespective of

---

[2] The judges variously relied on principles deriving from *Canada Steamship* and *contra proferentem*: we will see in a later chapter whether these principles are still live in the context of indemnities.

[3] In fact on appeal from the Scottish courts.

> *the cause of loss or damage, including where such loss or damage*
> *is caused by, or contributed to, by the negligence of [[Asco]]."*

The question before the court was whether the expression "defend, indemnify and hold harmless" could cover Asco's negligence: this was an action as between two parties to a contract. The court rejected the idea that such a clause was only aimed at giving protection against third party claims. As Lord Clarke put it,

> *"... in this charterparty the expression 'defend, indemnify and*
> *hold harmless' is wide enough both to provide a defence for one*
> *party to claims made by the other party and to provide an*
> *indemnity in respect of the claims of third parties."*

It will be seen from these two cases that two very senior courts have come to diametrically opposite views as to the meaning of one of the most basic expressions used in drafting indemnities.

The same can be said about "keep indemnified": lawyers frequently use this expression, but it has no fixed meaning, no line of case-law supporting any settled understanding of the term.

The mystery is that lawyers keep on using these expressions.

It goes wider than that. There is no standard terminology associated with indemnity drafting, so one can see in contracts and judgments the following pairings:

Indemnifier and indemnified

Indemnifier and indemnifiee

Indemnifying party and indemnified party

Indemnitor and indemnitee

Of course, if desired, one can also mix and match terms taken from different pairings or one could even take terms from the related spheres of guarantees and international trade:

Guarantor

Surety

Beneficiary or creditor

Debtor or principal debtor

The reality is that there is no fixed terminology, no general agreement or understanding even regarding what the parties to an indemnity should be called. This book will proceed by talking about an "indemnifier" on the one hand and an "indemnified" on the other in the interests of brevity and consistency. Where an indemnity is offered against the non-performance of some third party contract, that third party will be called a "debtor", as in cases relating to guarantees, and the third party contract will be referred to as the "underlying debt".

As to what indemnities themselves mean, it is the aim of this book to elucidate their meaning and effect.

The emergence of indemnities

It is perhaps strange that there is a dearth of agreement on terminology as the indemnity is by no means a modern creation of the law or of lawyers. There are statutes which make use of the concept e.g.

Partnership Act 1890 section 24(2) – a firm must indemnify a partner in respect of payments and liabilities incurred in the ordinary course of business or necessarily done to preserve the firm's business or property

Companies Act 2006 section 767(3) – the directors must indemnify a party to a transaction suffering loss as a result of trading in breach of section 761 (requirements as to minimum share capital)

Even without statutes, some relationships have been found to create a right to indemnity under the common law e.g.

An accommodation party to a bill of exchange is entitled to be indemnified by the party accommodated

An agent is entitled to indemnity from the principal against liabilities reasonably incurred in the performance of the contract of agency

An employee is similarly entitled to indemnity from an employer

The courts of Equity have also made use of the concept e.g.

A personal representative is entitled to indemnity out of the estate for expenses properly incurred

A trustee may be entitled to indemnity from co-trustees

Cases on some of these areas go back many, many years: the indemnity is by no means a modern invention.

When is an indemnity not an indemnity?
When it is a guarantee ...

Unfortunately, it is not possible to discuss indemnities without venturing into the thorny subject of how an indemnity differs from a guarantee. An introduction to the distinction can be seen in *Yeoman Credit Ltd v Latter* [1961] 1 WLR 828 where Harman LJ said that the distinction between a guarantee and an indemnity was,

> "... *a most barren controversy. It dates back ... to the Statute of Frauds, 1677, and has raised many hair-splitting distinctions of exactly that kind which brings the law into hatred, ridicule and contempt by the public ... and the decided cases on the subject are hardly to be reconciled.*"

Holroyd Pearce LJ in his judgment in the same case gave a beautifully simple summary of the distinction which perhaps belies the enormous amount of litigation on the subject both before and since his judgment,

> "*An indemnity is a contract by one party to keep the other harmless against loss, but a contract of guarantee is a contract to answer for the debt, default or miscarriage of another who is to be primarily liable to the promisee.*"

The mention of the Statute of Frauds 1677 above means we must look at what it says, using the quaint language and spelling to be found in the online version at legislation.gov.uk,

> "*IV No Action against Executors, &c. upon a special Promise, or upon any Agreement, or Contract for Sale of Lands, &c. unless Agreement, &c. be in Writing and signed.*

> *Noe Action shall be brought . . . whereby to charge the*
> *Defendant upon any speciall promise to answere for the debt*
> *default or miscarriages of another person . . . unlesse the*
> *Agreement upon which such Action shall be brought or some*
> *Memorandum or Note thereof shall be in Writeing and signed*
> *by the partie to be charged therewith or some other person*
> *thereunto by him lawfully authorized.* "

In general, the essence of a guarantee is that it is a secondary obligation, coextensive with the underlying debt being guaranteed, and is brought into play when the debtor defaults. This is what is meant in the 1677 Act by "answering for" a third party's "debts, defaults or miscarriages". If the debtor fails to pay £100 as required by a contract, then the guarantor of that debt becomes liable instead for £100.

As against which, an indemnity is a primary obligation, compensating the indemnified for defined losses or expenses described in the indemnity and the indemnity can become payable even without a third party's default, all depending on how the indemnity is worded.

One consequence of the distinction between a guarantee and an indemnity, and one which is the cause of most of the problems, is that a guarantee falling within the 1677 Act has to be in writing and signed. We can dispose fairly swiftly of the requirement of what constitutes writing and signature as the courts in recent times take a fairly expansive approach to this requirement, as shown in *Golden Ocean v Salgaocar* [2012] EWCA Civ 265. There was a ten year charterparty and Golden Ocean alleged that the other party had repudiated it causing US$54m of loss. Golden Ocean alleged that Salgaocar was the guarantor. In fact, the alleged guarantee was not to be found in a formal contract of guarantee, but rather in a chain of emails. The Court of Appeal made short shrift of the issue: an agreement of guarantee was not a special class of contract but was subject to the normal rules applying to contracts generally. This meant that a contract of guarantee could be found in a sequence of negotiating emails just as is the case with any commercial contract. As to signature, then this could be an electronic signature, or the first name, initials or perhaps just a nickname applied to an email (provided that it was clear as to the identity of the individual said to be "signing" the email).

But there has to be writing, and there has to be a signature, and these are the points which have bedevilled commercial parties who end up litigating in this area. Some examples will illustrate the point, if not make it clear.

In *Actionstrength v International Glass Engineering Limited* [2003] UKHL 17, Actionstrength provided labour only services to help build a unit for St Gobain under a contract with IGEL. Debt built up due to non-payment by IGEL. Actionstrength became more and more concerned at the non-payment and, at a meeting of senior representatives of all three parties, St Gobain orally agreed to ensure Actionstrength got paid. IGEL in fact went into insolvency owing Actionstrength around £1.3m. Actionstrength argued that the oral statement made by St Gobain amounted to some sort of estoppel which could circumvent the Statute of Frauds. The Court of Appeal had described this argument as "absolutely hopeless" and the House of Lords upheld that decision. The selfsame words could not be at the same time both an unenforceable guarantee and an estoppel overriding the statute.

For those interested, the judgment of the House of Lords contains an interesting history of the Statute of Frauds 1677, both in its original form and in its present, considerably truncated, form[4]. There is also consideration of the value of maintaining the requirement of writing and of the reports of the Law Commission on the subject. It is a difficult question: in a very real sense, a guarantee performs the same commercial function as an indemnity – it gives one party the assurance that it will get paid. We will look at this distinction again shortly when considering whether certain defences applicable to guarantees extend also to indemnities.

In *Pitts v Jones* [2007] EWCA Civ 1301, Pitts was an employee and minority shareholder in a company majority owned by Jones. Jones wanted to sell the shares in the company to a third party and reached a provisional agreement to do so. Jones told Pitts about this, the latter assuming that he would be paid cash for his shares. In fact the purchaser proposed to pay in instalments. Pitts was not happy about this proposal and, at an EGM called to deal with the matter, Jones orally assured Pitts that he would pay if the purchaser did not. The sale went through but the purchaser went into insolvency. Pitts sued Jones on his oral promise.

The Court of Appeal said that a guarantee was a type of indemnity, and that the term *"merely connotes the right of one party to look to another [to] satisfy his losses and may arise under a contract (for example under a contract of insurance) or by operation of law"*. The Court of Appeal out of these facts identified two separate transactions: firstly, there was the sale of Jones' shares to the purchaser and, secondly, there was Pitts' sale of his shares to the purchaser. Jones' oral assurance to Pitts was part of this second and separate transaction and could not be seen as part of a

---

[4] Originally, other transactions which required writing included contracts entered into in contemplation of marriage, for example.

larger unitary transaction. This being so, Jones' oral assurance was a guarantee within the 1677 Act and therefore unenforceable without writing.

A very recent example can be found in the case of *Abbhi v Slade* [2019] EWCA Civ 2175. Abbhi was funding his father-in-law's (Singh's) inheritance litigation. He was conscious of the risks of being found to be a third party funder of litigation and so was providing funds to Singh who then in turn paid for legal representation. Shortly before trial, a new solicitor was appointed to represent Singh, one Slade. Abbhi met Slade at a meeting without the presence of Singh. During that meeting, Abbhi agreed that he would pay Slade but would do so by putting Singh in funds so that Singh would be able to pay Slade. The engagement letter was entered into as between Singh and Slade, Abbhi was not mentioned. Singh went on to lose his case and died insolvent, owing Slade some £317,000 (of which some £250,000 consisted of unpaid counsels' fees). Abbhi meanwhile had stopped paying Singh. Was this a guarantee (oral – unenforceable) or an indemnity (potentially enforceable)?

The Court of Appeal found that,

> "*[t]he critical question which determines whether a contract is one of guarantee within section 4 of the Statute of Frauds is not that the promise is to pay another's debt but ... whether that promise is to pay if the other does not pay, in which case it is within the Statute of Frauds or whether it is a promise to put the claimant in funds in any event, in which case it is outside the Statute of Frauds.*"

In this case, Abbhi had assumed a primary obligation to make payments to Singh in any event, as the underlying agreement was to pay Slade's bills by the circuitous route of putting Singh in funds, meaning that payment was not dependent on Singh defaulting. The oral agreement was therefore enforceable.

Even from these cases, it can be seen that hair-splitting distinctions can be the basis for determining whether a particular agreement is classed as a guarantee (no signature: unenforceable) or an indemnity (potentially enforceable without signature). There are many, many more in the same vein. Indeed, going back to the lament of Harman LJ in *Yeoman Credit Ltd v Latter* [1961] 1 WLR 828 quoted above (*"a most barren controversy"*), judges find themselves having to deal with ever more convoluted factual scenarios and seeking to discern either a primary or a secondary obligation. For present purposes, in a book aimed at describing contractual indemnities, it is not necessary to give further examples of this distinction.

Practice point

For the ordinary practising lawyer's purposes, it suffices to say that if, during a meeting, a party says anything to the effect that he will pay if someone else does not, however it is phrased and whatever the exact proposed contractual structure, just bear in mind that this promise almost certainly needs to be reduced to writing and signed by the potentially paying party to make it enforceable.

What else distinguishes a guarantee from an indemnity?

Guarantees benefit from various defences that have been applied for many years by the courts although there is nothing expressly in the Statute of Frauds dealing with such defences. The origins of these various defences are obscure, probably based on eighteenth and nineteenth century judges being reluctant to make individuals liable under a guarantee, which had become a much used instrument both in trade and domestic arrangements, and thereby demonstrating a paternalistic approach to the law in order to protect the vulnerable.

To take one example which bulks large in any consideration of guarantees (and just possibly, indemnities – see below), a rule emerged which became known as the rule in *Holme v Brunskill* (1878) 3 QBD 495 (although this case is by no means the first instance of the rule being applied). The facts of the case illustrate the principle. Holme let a farm in Cumbria to George Brunskill, taking a guarantee from his brother, the defendant. One obligation in the lease was for the return of the flock of sheep located on the farm in good order and condition. Holme served an invalid notice to quit on George Brunskill and the parties negotiated a variation to their agreement, whereby George Brunskill surrendered a field and Holme reduced the rent by £10. Holme subsequently served a further, valid, notice to quit. At the end of the tenancy, it was found that the flock of sheep was reduced in number and had not been well cared for. Holme sued George Brunskill's brother on his guarantee.

The rule as stated by the court is this: if the parties to the underlying debt being guaranteed vary it in any way, the surety must be asked to agree. If the parties fail to secure the surety's specific agreement to the variation, assuming the variation is not manifestly insubstantial or does not actually benefit the surety, the surety will be discharged from all obligations under the guarantee.

The rule was already well established by the time *Holme v Brunskill* came to be decided, as can be seen from A Treatise on the Law of Principal and Surety by Edward Dix Pitman, published in 1840,

> *"And the surety will be held discharged, although it be proved that time was given, in consequence of the principal's inability to pay, or that no injury had accrued, or that it was manifestly for the surety's advantage: the surety himself being the proper judge of, and he alone has the right to determine, what is or is not for his benefit; thus if one be surety by bond for the debt of another payable at a given day, and the obligee take promissory notes payable at a subsequent period, or a bond conditioned for paying the same debt by instalments, he thereby discharges the surety."*

One question that comes up from time to time is whether these defences applicable in the case of guarantees apply also to indemnities. If you think about it, an indemnity performs the same commercial function as a guarantee – it ensures that someone gets paid at the end of the day. You would think that the same rules would apply to an indemnity, therefore.

This came up again recently in *GPP Big Field v Solar EPC Solutions* [2018] EWHC 2866 (Comm). Solar was the parent company of the original party, Prosolia, to five contracts for the construction of solar power generation units in the UK. Prosolia had entered into insolvency and GPP was proceeding against the parent company, Solar, under the parent company guarantee. The relevant provision read as follows,

> *"6.1 [Solar] guarantees the due and punctual performance by the Contractor of the Contractor's duties and obligations to [GPP] under this Agreement*
>
> *6.2 If the Contractor fails to observe and perform any of its duties or obligations to [GPP], [Solar] (as a separate and independent obligation and liability from its obligations and liabilities under this Agreement) shall indemnify [GPP] against all loss, debt,*

damage, interest, cost and expense incurred by [GPP] by reason of such failure or breach and shall pay to the [GPP], without any deduction or set-off, the amount of that loss, debt, damage, interest, cost and expense."

The court had first to decide whether this provision, taken as a whole, was a guarantee or an indemnity: as can be seen, it uses both words in two different clauses. Moreover, it can be seen that the obligation commences on the failure of Prosolia to observe or perform any obligations under the agreements with GPP – an indicator that it was a guarantee. On the other hand, it then goes on to offer an indemnity against "all loss, debt, damage, interest, cost and expense" incurred by GPP – this is potentially wider than Prosolia's original obligation, so looks more like an indemnity.

The court found that this was an indemnity, not a guarantee: firstly, the use of words such as "guarantee" or "indemnity" was not conclusive, only a pointer; secondly, the promise in clause 6.2 was described as *"a separate and independent obligation and liability"*, which pointed to its being an indemnity; thirdly, the mention of *"loss, debt, damage, interest, cost and expense incurred"* was a broad obligation, not co-extensive with the underlying contractual obligation of Prosolia, again pointing to an indemnity and, finally, guarantees have grown up with a large amount of boilerplate provisions seeking to circumvent defences such as the rule in *Holme v Brunskill*, and they were absent here, again indicating that the parties did not think this was a guarantee.

The court then turned to the argument that defences applicable to guarantees should nonetheless apply to an indemnity. Solar pointed to various changes that had allegedly been agreed in the performance of the contract by Prosolia, including re-routing of various cables. However, the court relied on a number of other recent decisions in this area to find that defences applicable specifically to guarantees do not apply to indemnities.

Another distinction – releases

This is another area where the legal treatment of a guarantee diverges from that of an indemnity.

In the case of a guarantee, if the creditor releases the debtor from the original obligation, that will in the ordinary course of things function to release the surety as well: the surety's obligation under a guarantee is co-extensive with that of the debtor. If the debtor owes nothing, then the surety should owe nothing.

This is not necessarily the same with an indemnity as all will depend on the wording of the indemnity itself. An indemnity is not intended in all cases to be co-extensive with some underlying debt, even where the indemnity is given in the context of providing e.g. a parent company guarantee. Take again the case of *GPP Big Field v Solar EPC Solutions* [2018] EWHC 2866 (Comm) above: the parent company's obligation was not expressed as being an obligation to do or pay whatever the insolvent subsidiary company should have done or paid (but now could not because of its insolvency); the parent company's obligation was to pay all "*loss, debt, damage, interest, cost and expense incurred by [the first claimant] by reason of such failure or breach [by the subsidiary]*". Reference to clause 6.2 set out above will show that this obligation was to be undertaken without deduction or set-off. It is easy to see that the damage caused by the insolvent subsidiary's failure might be greater than the obligation undertaken by the subsidiary itself: for example, if the subsidiary's contract with GPP allowed it to set off its own counterclaims against GPP, then Solar, the parent company, would be liable under the indemnity to pay sums without set-off or deduction that the subsidiary would never have been liable for.

This has important implications for parent company guarantees in particular, and we will return to this subject in the Chapter Six when dealing with indemnities covering breaches by third parties.

Practice point

For the moment, the important point is that an indemnity, at least when covering losses caused by a third party, needs to deal with the situation of what should happen where the third party is not or ceases to be liable for a breach of the obligation being indemnified against. Is the intention that the indemnifier should still be liable? This needs to be made clear. The point will be further illustrated in Chapter Six.

When is an indemnity not an indemnity? When it is an on demand obligation ...

This is another problem that bedevils the drafting of indemnities and is becoming a frequent subject of litigation. The use of language suggesting "on demand" payment or performance may well take an indemnity out of the scope of being considered an indemnity as such and make the obligation more closely resemble an on demand performance or payment bond as used typically in international trade. Some examples will make this distinction clear.

In *Ultrabulk A/S v Jagatramka* [2017] EWHC 2792 (Comm), Ultrabulk operated a fleet of vessels of which Gujarat was a customer for the purpose of shipping coke extracted in India. Jagatramka was the chairman and MD of Gujarat. By early 2013, Gujarat owed Ultrabulk around

US$4.25m. By an agreement in July 2013, Gujarat promised to pay the outstanding sum by the end of the year. Jagatramka signed a personal guarantee of which the material parts were as follows,

> "WHEREAS I, Mr Jagatramka (... the 'Guarantor') ... am aware of the Joint Venture Agreement between [[Ultrabulk]] and [[Gujarat]] dated [[date]].
>
> I am also aware of the liability due on [[date]], i.e. USD4,259,395/- to [[Ultrabulk]] by [[Gujarat]] under the Agreement (the 'Gujarat Liabilities').
>
> NOW, therefore, I, the Guarantor, hereby unconditionally and irrevocably guarantee that, if for any reason Gujarat do not repay the Gujarat Liabilities latest by 31 December 2013 then I will on [[Ultrabulk's]] first written demand ..., pay a sum equivalent to the Gujarat Liabilities plus the interest based on annual Libor plus 2% to [[Ultrabulk]].
>
> ... I irrevocably confirm that I will not contest and/or defend any application and/or proceedings to enforce this Personal Guarantee in England and Wales or elsewhere ..."

The evidence pointed to the fact that, by the end of 2013, Gujarat had managed to pay Ultrabulk just under half of the outstanding sum. Ultrabulk proceeded against Jagatramka under his guarantee. The question was whether his "guarantee" should be seen as a guarantee (in the Statute of Frauds sense) obliging him to make up the difference between what had been paid the original total of US$4.25m or as some sort of on-demand payment bond. The wording veers between the two: it is true that it uses the word "guarantee" but, as we have seen, this is not decisive. It does state that his liability only arises following a default by Gujarat, which makes it look like a guarantee but it does use the expression, "first written demand" and says that his liability is for the "Gujarat Liabilities", which is defined as being the total sum of US$4.25m.

The court had no hesitation in finding that this was not a "guarantee" in the true sense, but an on demand obligation to pay the sum of US$4.25m following default by Gujarat. If it had been a guarantee, then the principle of co-extensivity would have demanded that Jagatramka should only be liable to pay the outstanding amount owed by Gujarat, not the full amount.

This is an important point for drafting: as indemnities have become more common, lawyers have started to add in elements taken from international trade, and one of those elements is the use of "on demand" language. This can change the nature of an indemnity to compensate for certain defined expenses into an obligation simply to pay a fixed sum. Take for example the recent case of *AXA v Genworth Financial International* [2019] EWHC 3376 (Comm). AXA had acquired from Genworth two companies, FICL and FACL, which had been engaged in underwriting PPI insurance for store cards sold to consumers by Santander at retail outlets. As is well known, PPI complaints and claims in respect of mis-selling have become legion in recent years and the parties were well aware that AXA, in acquiring FICL and FACL, was taking on a potentially large and perhaps unquantifiable risk. They dealt with this by making Genworth liable for the majority of any liability in the following terms,

> *"The Sellers hereby covenant to the Purchaser and each Target Group Company that they will pay to the Purchaser or such Target Group Company on demand an amount equal to:*
>
> > *(a) ninety percent (90%) of all Relevant Distributor Mis-selling Losses; and*
> >
> > *(b) ninety percent (90%) of the amount of all costs, claims, damages, expenses or any other losses incurred by the Purchaser or a Target Group Company after Completion resulting from the Relevant Distributor Dispute or settlement thereof ... "*

Was this an indemnity? It does not use the word "indemnity" but simply states that a payment will be made "on demand" equal to 90% of certain defined sums. If it was an indemnity, would there be an implied obligation to run reasonable defences to all PPI mis-selling claims made against FICL and FACL so as to minimise any claims made under the indemnity?

The court declined to be led into categorising the clause by any particular label such as "indemnity" or to find that any particular obligations were to be implied following any such categorisation. The court's function was to apply the words contained in the contract. Genworth's obligation was set out clearly – it had to pay 90% of certain defined sums "on demand". The demand having been made, its obligation to pay had been triggered and there was no need to go behind the wording to find implied obligations qualifying that obligation to pay by making it subject to any conditions. We will come back to this case when looking at how indemnities are construed by the courts in Chapter Two.

The cases on this source of confusion are still coming in. Take the recent case of *Yuanda v Multiplex Construction* [2020] EWHC 468 (TCC): admittedly, not a case on an indemnity, but a useful case illustrating perhaps the general confusion in the drafting of instruments these days. Multiplex was the main contractor and Yuanda its subcontractor on the construction of the "Vase" in London (also referred to as the "Boomerang" or the "Tummy"). ANZ Banking Group took out a "Guarantee Bond" in favour of Multiplex. In fact, there were delays leading to Multiplex becoming liable to the employer and it sought to recover under the "Guarantee Bond". But what was it: a guarantee or a bond? Clause 1 provided,

> *"The Guarantor guarantees to the Contractor that in the event of a breach of the Contract by the Sub-Contractor, the Guarantor shall subject to the provisions of this Guarantee Bond satisfy and discharge the damages sustained by the Contractor as established and ascertained pursuant to and in accordance with the provisions of or by reference to the Contract and taking into account all sums due or to become due to the Sub-Contractor."*

Clause 5 provided,

> *"The Sub-Contractor, having requested the execution of this Guarantee Bond by the Guarantor, undertakes to the Guarantor (without limitation of any other rights and remedies of the Contractor or the Guarantor against the Sub-Contractor) to perform and discharge the obligations on its part set out in the contract."*

Was this an on demand bond entitling Multiplex to call on the "Guarantee Bond" and insist on immediate payment, or was it a guarantee, dependent on proving an underlying breach by Yuanda of the subcontract? The judge had no hesitation in ruling that it was a guarantee, not an on demand bond.

Having said all of which, there are cases where the expression "on demand" is used but the court still has construed the clause as an indemnity, and some examples will be seen later in this book. Using "on demand" does not inevitably mean that the clause is not an indemnity: it is simply another factor to be taken into account.

Practice point

Why are so many cases appearing on this issue? One problem is that, when coming to indemnities, lawyers tend to pile up empty phrases without thinking to set out in express language what exactly they want to achieve. The lesson coming out of these and other cases is clear: care needs to be taken when drafting indemnities to state exactly what is intended. Reliance should not be put on tired phrases such as "save and hold harmless", "guarantee", "on demand" and their ilk. The adviser for an indemnifier should ensure that the actual indemnity obligation does not slide into being some sort of on demand performance or payment bond or a guarantee. To put it bluntly: say what you mean.

When is an indemnity not an indemnity?
When it is not called one!

The title of this section is perhaps not strictly accurate: an indemnity can still function as an indemnity for most or even all practical purposes even though the parties have not used the word "indemnity". In a sense, it operates as what this book calls a "quasi-indemnity" – showing much the same if not all the attributes of an indemnity but simply not using that word. There are some advantages to proceeding in this way: many lawyers have become averse to accepting indemnities in commercial contracts. By using a different word or different words, but achieving the same result, it is possible to have an indemnity without wasting time on negotiations and re-drafts. A couple of examples will make this clear.

In *Arthur White v Tarmac* [1967] 1 WLR 1508, one Spalding was an engineer working with Thornaby-on-Tees local authority. Tarmac had a contract with Thornaby to carry out certain works on an airfield. Tarmac had entered into a contract with Arthur White to hire a digger together with a driver. While on site, the driver left the digger with its boom in an unsafe condition causing it to collapse on Spalding and causing him very serious injuries. The court found both Tarmac and Arthur White liable for their respective breaches of statutory duty, but the question then was whether Arthur White could recover against Tarmac for its share of the legal liability. The relevant clause in the hire contract read,

> *"Handling of Plant. 8. When a driver or operator is supplied by [Arthur White] to work the plant, he shall be under the direction and control of [Tarmac]. Such drivers or operators shall for all purposes in connection with their employment in the working of the plant be regarded as the servants or agents of [Tarmac] who alone shall be responsible for all claims arising in connection with the operation of the plant by the said drivers or operators."*

Notwithstanding the absence of the word "indemnity", the House of Lords appears to have proceeded on the basis that this wording achieved the same effect, Lord Pearce commenting that the parties can apportion liability under a contract as they wish, and there is no room to imply words apportioning liability under an indemnity. The result was that the court declined to limit the effect of clause 8 – it was designed to achieve the result that Tarmac bore the sole responsibility for wrongs (including negligence) done to third parties (like Spalding) occurring during the duration of the contract.

A more recent example can be seen in *Mir Steel v Morris* [2012] EWCA Civ 1397. Mir Steel had been created to receive the assets of an insolvent company in a sale by the administrators (Morris). That insolvent company some years previously had entered into a contract with Lictor Anstalt for the construction of a hot strip mill that was installed on its premises. The terms were perhaps unusual in that Lictor Anstalt retained title to all materials comprising the mill itself. When the administrators came to sell the company's assets to Mir Steel, they were on notice that Lictor Anstalt was asserting its rights to the hot strip mill. The contract of sale between the administrators and Mir Steel provided,

> "[Mir Steel] agrees that it shall be responsible for settling any claim made against it by Lictor Anstalt in respect of the hot strip mill situated at the Property."

Lictor Anstalt did indeed make claims in respect of its property rights, and further claimed in conversion and inducement of breach of contract. Should the words "any claim" be given a restrictive meaning or should they cover all and any claims made by Lictor Anstalt?

The Court of Appeal had no hesitation in finding that the expression should be given its ordinary meaning – it really did mean "any claim", regardless of what that claim was or what legal theory was invoked as the basis of the claim. In other words, this was an indemnity in all but name.

While it is fair to say that the same result may be achieved by replacing the word "indemnity" with an equivalent obligation, there is the risk that one benefit of the indemnity may be lost, namely, the indemnifier's right to be subrogated to any claim of the indemnified against a third party. It is worth noting the comments of the judge in *AXA v Genworth Financial International* [2019] EWHC 3376 (Comm) at paragraph 119,

> "The language used in Clause 10.8 and associated definitions is not 'to indemnify' but to 'covenant to pay....on demand' i.e. to make a promise to pay on demand – the demand being the trigger to require payment. If the parties had intended the obligation to be a contractual obligation to indemnify they would have so stated."

One consequence of the wording in that case being construed as an on demand payment obligation and not an indemnity was that the right of subrogation could not be engaged. This risk should be borne in mind when drafting "quasi-indemnities": the court may give effect to them as indemnities and thereby preserve a right of subrogation in appropriate cases, or the failure to use that word may deprive the indemnifier of any right of subrogation. It is another area where the paucity of authority in the area of indemnities leads to some uncertainty in their application.

Also note the discussion below of *Total Transport Corp v Arcadia Petroleum (The Eurus)* [1998] 1 Lloyds Rep 351 (CA), another case where a clause dealt with liability without using the word "indemnity": the Court of Appeal struggled to comprehend what was meant by the wording used, declining in the end to enforce the clause as a full indemnity, rather construing it as a more limited right to compensation (which was in fact denied on the unusual facts in that case): see below for a fuller discussion of this unusual case.

And finally: when else is an indemnity not an indemnity?
When the contract says nothing about it ...

The heading is perhaps confusing: this section deals with the situation where there is no indemnity drafted into the contract but the court finds grounds to imply one.

The common law may imply an indemnity in some circumstances. In *Sheffield Corporation v Barclay* [1905] AC 392 (HL) Timbrell and Honnywill owned a corporation. Timbrell fraudulently forged Honnywill's signature on stock transfers and borrowed money from Barclay putting up the forged transfers as security. Barclay requested the corporation to register it as holder of the stock, which the corporation duly did. Barclay transferred the stock on to third parties, with the corporation issuing fresh certificates as requested. Being purchasers for value, those transferees gained rights as against the corporation. Timbrell died and the fraud was discovered: Honnywill caused the corporation to restore the stock at some considerable expense. Could the corporation recover from Barclay?

The answer of the House of Lords was that it could: Barclay had requested the corporation to do a purely ministerial act in registering a transfer and issuing fresh certificates. Barclay, as the bank, was in a position to make proper enquiries which would have uncovered the fraud whereas the corporation was simply complying with instructions. Lord Halsbury stated the principle,

> *"It is a general principle of law when an act is done by one person at the request of another, which act is not in itself manifestly tortious to the knowledge of the person doing it, and such act turns out to be injurious to the rights of a third party, the person doing it is entitled to an indemnity from him who requested that it should be done."*

While the facts may seem somewhat extreme, it is still a lively doctrine and capable of being applied by the courts, as shown in *Triad Shipping v Stellar Chartering (the Island Archon)* [1994] 2 Lloyds Rep 227 (CA). Triad chartered the Island Archon to Stellar which sub-chartered her to a third party. The vessel was ordered to go to Basrah where SEMA was the local agent which had to be used by all vessels. What then happened became known in the trade as the "Iraqi System": SEMA would require security against claims of short loading or damage, which were routinely upheld by the courts giving judgment to the cargo receivers. The request for security was the cause of the vessel's delay in leaving Basrah. The facts as found by the arbitrator were as follows: the "Iraqi System" was not well known at the time of chartering and, furthermore, there was no significant loss or damage to the cargo so the claims made by the Basrah cargo receivers were highly suspect. Was the time charterer responsible for indemnifying the owners of the vessel in respect of the losses suffered by paying SEMA and the cargo receivers at Basrah?

The Court of Appeal found support for the idea of an implied indemnity from the *Sheffield Corporation* case but thought that a time charterer could not be responsible for everything under either an express or implied indemnity. As a general approach, the owners will be taken to accept the ordinary incidents of undertaking a voyage such that the implied indemnity of a time charterer would not cover normal risks – it exists for unusual risks which are not known or appreciated by the vessel's owner when entering into the charterparty. As the "Iraqi System" was not understood at the time of the charter, the owners of the vessel could not be taken to have accepted the risk of being liable to SEMA and the cargo receivers at Basrah.

There is an irony here: in an ordinary contractual claim for damages, the defendant would only be liable for the loss naturally arising in the ordinary course of things[5]. On the other hand, when considering the applicability of an implied indemnity, the very opposite was held to apply: the indemnifier would only be liable for losses which were not those naturally arising in the ordinary course of things; in other words, the indemnifier would only be liable for the unexpected.

However, too much should not be read into the cases on implied indemnities. In *Ben Shipping v An Bord Bainne* [1986] 2 All ER 177, Ben Shipping, owners of the "C Joyce", entered into a charterparty with An Bord Bainne, which wanted to transport powdered milk products to South Africa. The charterparty excluded the owner's liability for cargo damage except for its *"want of due diligence ... or default"* but included a "clause paramount", incorporating the Hague Rules into any bill of lading transferring ownership of the cargo to subsequent purchasers. The Hague Rules imposed liability on the shipowner without the carve out for due diligence or default. The charterer negotiated the bills of lading to new purchasers in the course of transit and the shipowner subsequently faced claims for damage to the cargo from the new cargo

---

[5] The first limb of the rule in *Hadley v Baxendale* [1854] EWHC J70

owners. Here was a conundrum: while the shipowner had effectively limited its liability for claims from the charterer in the charterparty, as soon as the charterer had negotiated the bills of lading to a new purchaser, the new purchaser faced no such limitation as it could rely on the Hague Rules.

The shipowner settled the claims made by the purchasers of the cargo and then sought an implied indemnity from the charterer. The shipowner failed. Bingham J found that the charterparty was specific in providing for the master of the vessel to be empowered to issue bills of lading incorporating the Hague Rules according to the "clause paramount", just as it was specific in limiting the charterer's claims against the shipowner to situations where the shipowner was in default or had failed to show due diligence. The parties may have realised this inconsistency or (more likely) never gave a moment's thought to it. It meant that the shipowner had a defence against the charterer which it could not use against a subsequent purchaser of the cargo from the charterer. It was a bad deal from the shipowner's point of view. However, this was no reason to imply an indemnity that the shipowner should be reimbursed for the defence and settlement of claims made by subsequent purchasers of the cargo.

Undoubtedly, there are some relationships where an indemnity will be more readily implied (such as the right to indemnity of a master of a vessel for following the instructions of a charterer), but the conditions for implying terms in the modern law of contract are very hard to satisfy and it may well be that the principle illustrated in *Sheffield Corporation v Barclay* is of much more limited application in the modern law. For example, in *Priminds Shipping v Noble Chartering* [2020] EWHC 127 (Comm), Noble was the time charterer of a vessel which in turn chartered the vessel to Priminds for the purpose of carrying goods from Brazil to China. On arrival, they were found to be defective causing the shipowner to pay US$1m to the Chinese receivers of the cargo. Noble settled the owner's claim for contribution in the sum of US$500,000 and then sought to recover this sum by way of an implied indemnity from Priminds. The bill of lading was subject to the Hague Rules, which provided for no express indemnity in these circumstances: they provided for an indemnity from the charterer in respect of information supplied by it but not in the case of any obligation arising from the apparent order and condition of the cargo.

The judge observed that it was hard to satisfy the test of necessity for implying terms[6], especially in a professionally drafted agreement[7]. The Hague Rules were highly sophisticated and provided for risk allocation as between the parties. As they did not provide for compensation in the situation which had happened, it was not possible to imply an indemnity to plug the gap: the conclusion was that the loss simply lay where it fell and Noble was not entitled to recover its loss from Priminds.

While this book has described the concept of an implied indemnity as "lively", too much reliance should not be placed on it, given the strict approach adopted by modern courts to the implication of terms, as shown in the *Priminds* case above. In the modern law, an implied indemnity is more likely to appear as an allegation in a pleading than as a finding in a judgment.

---

[6] *Marks and Spencer v BNP Paribas* [2015] UKSC 72

[7] See for example *UTB LLC v Sheffield United Limited* [2019] EWHC 2322 (Ch)

CHAPTER TWO
CONSTRUCTION OF
INDEMNITIES

"... every contract must be construed in accordance with its terms and little assistance is given by seeking to pigeonhole a contract into any particular type of provisions such as whether it is in the nature of a contract of indemnity."[8]

In a very real sense, nearly all cases on indemnities are about construction, as each case will depend on the very words used in the indemnity seen in context to determine the applicability of that indemnity to the events that have occurred. What follows in this chapter takes a look at the general approach to construction used in English Law today with special reference to indemnities and also looks at some possibly unique elements applicable to indemnities as a class. Later chapters are also largely about construction as they look at specific indemnity clauses, but they illustrate specific, not general, points.

Ordinary rules of construction

It is not for nothing that the latest and greatest case to come out of the Supreme Court on the topic of construing contracts in general deals with

---

[8] *AXA v Genworth Financial International Holdings* [2019] EWHC 3376 (Comm), paragraph 118

an indemnity – *Wood v Capita Insurance Services* [2017] UKSC 24. We will look at this case presently but for the moment we will simply observe that nowhere in the Supreme Court's judgment is there any reference to the fact that an indemnity needs to have applied to it any special rules of construction.

This was illustrated recently by a case we have looked at above in Chapter One, *AXA v Genworth Financial International* [2019] EWHC 3376 (Comm). It will be recalled that the case concerned a clause in a share purchase agreement. The companies being sold had been involved in underwriting PPI insurance for store cards sold by Santander through retail outlets and accordingly there was a genuine fear that the companies being sold to AXA faced large liabilities in respect of PPI mis-selling complaints and claims. These in fact materialised and had to be dealt with by the companies who contracted with Santander to handle the numerous claims which arose. There is a strict regulatory regime dealing with how such complaints and claims should be handled, the overall position being that they should not be dealt with in a strictly legalistic or adversarial way. The clause in question provided that the seller, Genworth, covenanted to "*pay to [AXA] ... on demand an amount equal to*" 90% of the losses, costs, claims, damages and expenses incurred by AXA in disposing of the PPI mis-selling claims.

One line of defence put forward by Genworth was that the relevant clause should be seen as an indemnity and, that being so, there should be implied into the obligation to indemnify further ancillary obligations on AXA, including that it should advance all defences reasonably available to it in dealing with PPI mis-selling complaints and claims. The argument was that, to the extent that AXA did not advance all such defences, then the indemnity should not apply.

The court did not accept this line of argument. As can be seen from the quotation from the judgment opening this Chapter, the court did not accept that the right way to proceed was by first categorising the clause in dispute and then applying certain fixed characteristics to the clause as so categorised. The correct approach was to construe the words as used by the parties and then to apply them to the facts. In this case, the court found that the words were not in the form of an indemnity but rather a covenant to pay certain sums on demand. In other words, as soon as the demand was made, the obligation to pay arose. The parties had simply not provided that AXA should advance all defences reasonably available to it in dealing with PPI mis-selling claims: they could have done so but obviously had not. The strict test of necessity for implying terms had not been met[9].

Turning to *Wood v Capita Insurance Services* [2017] UKSC 24, Wood was the vendor to Capita of his shares in Sureterm, a company that had been providing insurance services to owners of classic cars. Prior to the sale, Sureterm had been operating by providing online quotations. When customers rang Sureterm to confirm the quotation they had received online, some telephone sales agents would then go on to provide higher quotations or to pressurise customers into accepting inflated quotations.

After the sale to Capita, an internal review uncovered the practice and Capita decided that it would self-report to the FSA. A subsequent investigation concluded that affected customers should be contacted and compensation offered to them. This was a substantial sum together with the costs of administering the compensation scheme and Capita wished to claim it from Wood. Capita was out of time to make a claim under the

---

[9] *Marks & Spencer Plc v BNP Paribas* [2015] UKSC 72

various warranties included in the share purchase agreement, but there was an indemnity in these terms,

> *"The Sellers undertake to pay to the Buyer an amount equal to the amount which would be required to indemnify the Buyer and each member of the Buyer's Group against all actions, proceedings, losses, claims, damages, costs, charges, expenses and liabilities suffered or incurred, and all fines, compensation or remedial action or payments imposed on or required to be made by the Company following and arising out of claims or complaints registered with the FSA, the Financial Services Ombudsman or any other Authority against the Company, the Sellers or any Relevant Person and which relate to the period prior to the Completion Date pertaining to any mis-selling or suspected mis-selling of any insurance or insurance related product or service."*

The very prolixity of this wording, with its numerous terms, sub-clauses and intermittent punctuation, forbids easy comprehension. The Supreme Court described it as "avoidably opaque", which seems a polite way of putting it. But what did it mean?

Capita tried to get around the complexity of the wording by breaking it down into two separate indemnities:

- all actions, proceedings, losses, claims, damages, costs, charges, expenses and liabilities suffered or incurred AND

- all fines, compensation or remedial action or payments imposed on or required to be made by the Company following and arising out of claims or complaints registered with the FSA, the Financial Services Ombudsman or any other Authority against the Company, the Sellers or any Relevant Person

Each of these separate indemnities is then subject to the closing words of the clause,

> *"... which relate to the period prior to the Completion Date pertaining to any mis-selling or suspected mis-selling of any insurance or insurance related product or service."*

In other words, the crucial words they wanted to rely on would read,

> *"all actions, proceedings, losses, claims, damages, costs, charges, expenses and liabilities suffered or incurred ... which relate to the period prior to the Completion Date pertaining to any mis-selling or suspected mis-selling of any insurance or insurance related product or service."*

Wood took a very different approach. His argument was that there was in reality one long indemnity thus,

> *"all actions, proceedings, losses, claims, damages, costs, charges, expenses and liabilities suffered or incurred [[as well as]] all fines, compensation or remedial action or payments imposed on or required to be made by the Company ..."*

However, he argued, all of this wording was subject to the remaining words of the clause,

> *"... following and arising out of claims or complaints registered with the FSA, the Financial Services Ombudsman or any other Authority against the Company, the Sellers or any Relevant Person and which relate to the period prior to the Completion Date pertaining to any mis-selling or suspected mis-selling of any insurance or insurance related product or service"*

According to Wood's view, <u>any</u> claim for indemnity under this clause would have to follow and arise out of a claim or complaint against Sureterm. On his case, there was no claim or complaint against Sureterm – Capita had caused Sureterm to self-report. On its very words therefore, according to Wood, the indemnity simply did not apply to what had happened.

The Supreme Court did not find it easy to construe such a long and complex provision. The judgment is mostly concerned with the correct modern approach to construction of commercial contracts and is therefore outside the scope of this little book. The court talked about both a textual and a contextual approach: a textual (or literal) approach may be more useful when construing a professionally drafted document but, even then, the court acknowledged that the parties' conflicting aims, failures of communication, differing drafting practices or deadlines compelling compromise during negotiation might each lead to a document that was not internally consistent or coherent. Where a document is unclear or where it is not professionally drafted, then a more contextual approach may be appropriate – an approach therefore taking account of the factual matrix.

The important point for present purposes is that the Supreme Court took account of the other provisions in the agreement in order to construe this indemnity. They noted the presence of time-limited warranties, as is common in corporate transactions. It made sense to have wide-ranging warranties, which were subject to a time-limit for any warranty claims, but then to have an indemnity without a time-limit for bringing claims but which could only be triggered in certain specific circumstances. While at first sight it might seem anomalous to have an indemnity that applied to claims brought by third parties but not in the case of self-reporting, it made more sense when viewing the indemnity in the wider context of the agreement as a whole where there were wide-ranging warranties, albeit subject to time-limits for bringing a claim under them. In other words, the indemnity should be seen as part of the wider risk allocation mechanism contained in the total contract.

The point to note about the judgement is that it leaves open both a "textual" and a "contextual" approach. True, each might be more appropriate in different situations, but both are alive as approaches to discerning meaning. In fact, what appears to have happened over the years is that the courts have – by and large – retreated from a contextual approach preferring to adopt a textual approach wherever possible. This can be seen too in indemnities, as the discussion of any of the modern indemnity cases in this book demonstrates.

A recent example at first instance is *Gwynt Y Môr v Gwynt Y Môr Offshore Wind Farm* [2020] EWHC 850 (Comm) where the claimant was the buyer of a business in maintaining and operating certain electrical transmission links. Part of the assets transferred were various undersea cables. Unknown to the parties, at the time of entering into the sale agreement, the cables suffered from a latent manufacturing defect which allowed seawater to enter the cables causing corrosion over the course of several months or even years. Shortly after completion, two of the cables in fact failed and the claimant had to see to repairs costing some £15 million. The relevant indemnity read,

> *"If any of the Assets are destroyed or damaged prior to Completion (Pre-Completion Damage), then, following Completion, the [defendants] shall indemnify the [claimant] against the full cost of reinstatement of any Assets affected by Pre-Completion Damage."*

The question was whether the claimant could recover under that indemnity: did it refer to damage or destruction occurring at any time, even prior to the sale agreement itself? Phillips LJ sitting at first instance found that *"... prior to Completion ..."* did not include damage occurring in the period before the sale agreement. The use of the words, *"are destroyed or damaged"* did not naturally refer to pre-existing damage: it would be more natural to say, *"if any of the Assets have been destroyed or damaged ..."* and even then it might be thought necessary to put the matter beyond doubt by adding e.g. *"including before this Agreement"*. On a straight reading, the indemnity covered damage occurring between the date of the execution of the agreement and completion.

So much for the textual approach, but the court also considered the context of the indemnity itself, where it appeared in the agreement (nestled in clauses dealing with the period between execution and completion) and the relation it bore to the warranty provisions. The parties had included complex warranties dealing with damage to the assets transferred, but these were hedged about with restrictions including that damage had to be "discovered" by the sellers and any claims being subject to minimum figures. It would not make sense, so the court thought, to have warranties subject to complex restrictions while at the same time including a broad indemnity would allow the claimant to recover for historic damage regardless.

Example of a textual approach to an indemnity

In *Transocean Drilling v Providence Resources* [2016] EWCA Civ 372, Transocean chartered a drilling rig to Providence on a time charterparty in a standard form known as "LOGIC" (suitably adapted by the parties). The judge found that the rig was defective on delivery and broke down causing delay and consequent losses (known in the case as "spread costs"). It will be readily understood that having personnel and equipment standing idle while an essential drilling rig is being repaired is an expensive affair.

The contract contained complex liability provisions but, for present purposes, it is necessary to note the lengthy definition of "consequential loss" including

> *"... loss of use (including, without limitation, loss of use or the cost of use of property, equipment, materials and services including without limitation, those provided by contractors or subcontractors of every tier or by third parties), loss of business and business interruption ..."*

Clause 20 contained mutual undertakings given by each party to indemnify the other against any claims for consequential loss. It was further provided that all the indemnities applied irrespective of cause and notwithstanding the negligence, breach of duty or other failure of the indemnified and irrespective of any claim that might otherwise arise in law[10].

This meant, of course, that Providence could effectively recover nothing in respect of the "spread costs": these were the costs of the downtime and other wasted expenses incurred through the rig's breakdown. They were, thought the Court of Appeal, exactly the sort of losses that were

---

[10] This rather strange formula of providing for mutual indemnities amounted to, as the court noted, an exclusion of liability for consequential loss (as defined): it is a very common approach in e.g. the construction and engineering industries and will be examined in Chapter Six when looking at indemnities against claims made by the indemnifier.

included in the definition of "consequential loss" above. One argument put forward by Providence was that this would effectively reduce the contract to nothing more than a "statement of intent" and that the court should strive to interpret the contract in some way that would allow Providence to recover its losses. At first instance, these arguments were successful but they failed before the Court of Appeal. As Moore-Bick LJ put it,

> "... I can see no reason in principle why commercial parties should not be free to embark on a venture of this kind on the basis of an agreement that losses arising in the course of the work will be borne in a certain way and that neither should be liable to the other for consequential losses, however they choose to define them. In my view the language of clause 20 is clear and is apt to exclude liability for wasted costs in the form of the spread costs which Providence seeks to recover in this case."

Example of a contextual approach to an indemnity

In *Caledonia North Sea v British Telecommunications* [2002] UKHL 4, the appeal to the House of Lords arose out of the Piper Alpha disaster leading to multiple claims by those injured or bereaved for compensation. As was noted in connection with the *Transocean* case above, being a case in the engineering sector, the contractual provisions considered by the court contained a large number of mutual indemnities. Why should this be? The House of Lords noted a number of factors in the factual matrix which determined why this approach was universally adopted:

1. The operations were potentially hazardous in the absence of rigorous safety precautions
2. Much of the work involved contractors and subcontractors

3. The regulatory regime that has emerged over the years to govern the exploration for oil makes the operator liable but, unlike the regulatory regime in the nuclear field, the operator of an offshore installation is not obliged to insure and there is no statutory inhibition of any right of indemnity or subrogation which might arise between the operator or the operator's insurer and any other party

The result of this was noted by the House of Lords as being that those involved in working in offshore installations adopted mutual indemnities to the effect that each employer would be left responsible for its own employees. This had manifest benefits for all concerned, not least an injured employee who needed only to look for compensation from his employer without having to make claims for compensation against the operator, where the operator might well seek contribution from third parties. This use of reciprocal indemnities thereby removed the complexity for all parties, not least the injured employee. The House of Lords proceeded to construe the contractual indemnities in the light of this established practice in the offshore installation industry and taking account of the aims described above of having reciprocal indemnities.

Indemnity or guarantee or demand bond?
Approaches to construction

In keeping with the general principles so far described, the courts do not approach indemnities by trying to categorise them either as indemnities or as any other sort of obligation. In *AXA v Genworth Financial International* [2019] EWHC 3376 (Comm), we saw that the court declined to categorise a provision as an indemnity and then attach a series of characteristics or implied terms to the provision being considered in virtue of its category as an indemnity. Some cases on guarantees are instructive, however, of the approach of the courts where the document they have to review is ambivalent as to its effect.

Let us first look briefly at *Marubeni v Mongolian Government* [2005] EWCA Civ 395. This concerned the purchase by a Mongolian company of machinery to be used in a cashmere processing plant. It was under a "Deferred Payment Purchase Contract", whereby the purchase price of some US$18.8m would be paid over a number of years. The contract provided for a "guarantee" to be provided by the Mongolian government, which it did. There were disputes over the quality of the machinery supplied and the purchaser fell behind with payment. The seller proceeded against the Mongolian government under the guarantee. In its material parts, that guarantee read,

> "... [Mongolia] unconditionally pledges to pay to you upon your simple demand all amounts payable under the Agreement if not paid when the same becomes due (whether at stated maturity, by acceleration or otherwise) and further pledges the full and timely performance and observance by the Buyer of all the terms and conditions of the Agreement. Further [Mongolia] undertakes to hold indemnify and hold you harmless from and against any cost and damage which may be incurred by or asserted against you in connection with any obligations of the Buyer to pay any amount under the Agreement when the same becomes due and payable (whether at stated maturity, by acceleration or otherwise) or to perform or observe any term or condition of the Agreement or in connection with any invalidity or unenforceability of or impossibility of performance of any such obligations of the Buyer. ... "

The Court of Appeal had difficulty with the baffling array of terminology used not only in the document before it, but more generally to describe different types of transactions, especially those in the international trade arena: the document referred to itself as a "guarantee" but it also contained the word "demand" (which suggested demand or performance bonds, also known as performance guarantees). To make matters worse, the document also contained an "indemnity" in the words following the "guarantee". So the question was, what was this document's effect? Did it take effect as a bond, i.e. an undertaking to pay a certain amount against the happening of an event or the presentation of certain documents (as commonly used by banks to support international transactions), or was it a true guarantee, i.e. a secondary obligation (sometimes referred to as a "see to it" guarantee)?

The Court of Appeal reviewed some of the cases in the area of demand bonds and noted that they concerned banks. This was not a case concerning a bank and, in the view of the Court of Appeal, without express language making it clear that the document was intended to take effect as some sort of demand bond, then there was *"a strong presumption"* against the document being construed in that way.

The next question then was whether there was anything in the document to displace that presumption. While the document did say *"unconditionally pledges"* and *"simple demand"* the wording was immediately qualified by the following words, which required default by the purchaser before the obligation to pay should arise: these words strongly suggested some sort of "see to it" guarantee. It then talked about pledging *"... the full and timely performance and observance by the buyer of all the terms and conditions of the agreement"*: again, this was the language of a secondary obligation – of a "see to it" guarantee, not a demand bond.

The Court of Appeal therefore concluded that the obligation was in fact a guarantee, not a demand bond. The case could be compared with *Wuhan Guoyu Logistics Group v Emporiki Bank of Greece SA* [2012] EWCA Civ 1629 where the Court of Appeal again had to struggle to construe a document which veered between the language of a guarantee and that of a demand bond, but finding this time that the document was a bond: the identity of the defendant bank as a bank was crucial. International transactions were underpinned by the work of banks and the reliance the commercial community can put on a demand bond being met by the bank. The Court of Appeal approved a passage from Paget's Law of Banking (11th Edition),

> *"Where an instrument (i) relates to an underlying transaction between the parties in different jurisdictions, (ii) is issued by a bank, (iii) contains an undertaking to pay "on demand" (with or without the words "first" and/or "written") and (iv) does not contain clauses excluding or limiting the defences available to a guarantor, it will almost always be construed as a demand guarantee. ..."*

Both of these cases were considered recently in *Rubicon Vantage v Krisenergy* [2019] EWHC 2012 (Comm). Rubicon chartered a "Floating Storage and Offloading Facility" to a company whose parent, Krisenergy, provided a guarantee. That guarantee was not in a completely conventional form, as it provided for undisputed sums to be payable within 48 hours of demand. Where a sum was disputed, then Krisenergy

"... shall be obliged to pay any amount(s) demanded up to a maximum amount of United States Dollars Three Million (US$3,000,000) on demand; ..."

Beyond the US$3m, Krisenergy was entitled to withhold the sum allegedly due until final determination of the dispute.

As the judge observed, reading the "guarantee" as a whole, it contained elements of both a true "see to it" guarantee (or secondary obligation), such as is normally used by parent companies, while it also contained elements of a demand or performance bond, such as is typically used by banks in international commerce. Krisenergy argued that, in the light of the authorities discussed immediately above[11], there was some sort of presumption or perhaps "approach" that a business operating outside the banking sphere would be most unlikely to enter into a demand bond and that the document should therefore be seen as a guarantee.

The court disagreed. The law does not approach a document with set presumptions seeking to find a particular result; rather, the court had to construe the words in the document in front of it. Any presumption deriving from *Marubeni* is aimed at deciding whether a document is either a "see to it" guarantee or a demand bond, but if the language is clear, there is no further use for the presumption and it becomes a simple matter of applying the words of the document. There was no presumption or rule of law to the effect that a non-bank could not enter into a demand bond. That being so, it was clear on the face of the document that the parties had in fact entered into a demand bond,

---

[11] *Marubeni Hong Kong v Mongolian Government* [2005] EWCA Civ 395; *Wuhan Guoyu Logistics Group v Emporiki Bank of Greece SA* [2012] EWCA Civ 1629

notwithstanding that they were operating in the energy, not the banking, sector.

There are many examples of this sort of confusion where lawyers have simply confounded matters by their sloppy use of terminology. To take but one more example, we can briefly consider the case of *Multiplex Construction v Dunne* [2017] EWHC 3073 (TCC). Dunne's company, DBCE, was in serious financial difficulties and Multiplex agreed to make a large advance payment (at first £3 million, later £4 million) against a "guarantee" given by Dunne in order to keep DBCE afloat. DBCE was important as it was engaged in vital sub-contracts for Multiplex. Dunne was described in the document as "Guarantor".

One relevant clause provided at clause 3.1,

> *"The Guarantor irrevocably and unconditionally guarantees, warrants and undertakes jointly and severally to [Multiplex] that should [DBCE] suffer an event of insolvency (including but not limited to administration, administrative receivership, liquidation, ceasing or threatening to ceasing carrying on its business in the normal course or otherwise) ... the Guarantor shall immediately be liable to [Multiplex] for the payment of the Advance Payment and shall indemnify and hold harmless [Multiplex] against any loss, damage, demands, charges, payments, liability, proceedings, claims, costs and expenses suffered or incurred by [Multiplex] arising therefrom or in connection therewith."*

This wording has cleverly combined the language not only of a guarantee, but also the language of warranties and undertakings whilst ingeniously finishing with a flourish by its mention of "indemnify and hold harmless".

But what is it? Fish or foul – a guarantee or an indemnity? Or perhaps neither – maybe it is something completely different? What is the effect of the wording and why could the draftsman not make it clear?

Fraser J rejected an approach based on *contra proferentem* citing from *Persimmon Homes v Ove Arup* [2017] EWCA Civ 373, which itself cited *Transocean Drilling v Providence Resources* [2016] EWCA Civ 372. He accepted that *contra proferentem* had a very limited role in construing modern contracts, and there was no need to single out guarantees or indemnities as beneficiaries of a stricter construction in favour of the guarantor or indemnifier. Ordinary rules of construction were to be used.

That being so, the words provided that Dunne would have to make good the advance payment if there were an act of insolvency, as broadly defined in the above wording. In that event, Dunne would *"immediately be liable to [Multiplex] for the payment of the Advance Payment"*. Note that the payment had to be made "immediately", which Fraser J found crucial. There was no accounting process to be undertaken – the full amount would have to be paid by Dunne to Multiplex. Again, there was no point imposing a primary obligation on DBCE to make the payment, as the event concerned DBCE's insolvency, when there would be no question of its making a payment of any sort. The commercial purpose of the agreement was to make Dunne liable as primary obligor, in other words as an indemnifier, to pay what DBCE could not pay and to do so immediately.

The final wording (*"shall indemnify and hold harmless"*) simply reinforced the judge's conclusion.

Practice point

Of course, some of the above cases concerned guarantees, not indemnities, but use of the wrong terminology has the potential to create confusion when it comes to enforcement. Increasingly, it would seem from the law reports, indemnities are using the language both of guarantees and demand bonds, leading to misunderstandings as to how they should be applied in practice. Far from making it easier to enforce the clause in question, it simply raises serious questions as to what exactly the wording means. The better course is to make it clear on the face of the document exactly what result is intended rather than to pile up phrases that obfuscate, rather than illuminate, the true (intended) meaning.

Literalness – the death (or life support) of *contra proferentem*

A principle of construction well known to older lawyers is that known as *"contra proferentem"* – the principle that a limitation, and especially an exclusion, of liability should be construed against the interests of the one relying on it. In fact, the *proferens* could be one of a number of people, including the one relying on it and the one that wrote it in the first place: for present purposes, let us assume that the principle applies to the one relying on it.

As mentioned above, the courts have moved much more closely towards a literalistic approach to construing contracts in recent years. This change of approach has been mirrored in the approach to limitations and exclusions of liability where, in recent years, we have seen the courts turning away from sometimes strained constructions of liability clauses in favour of simply applying them as they stand.

We have already mentioned *Transocean Drilling v Providence Resources* [2016] EWCA Civ 372, where the Court of Appeal (but not the trial judge) had no hesitation in upholding mutual indemnities having the effect of constituting mutual exclusions of liability for consequential loss as defined even though that meant that the claimant would in effect be deprived of a valuable claim. The trial judge had explicitly proceeded on the basis of applying the principle of *contra proferentem* so as to circumvent such a result as would leave the claimant unrecompensed. Moore-Bick LJ giving the judgment of the Court of Appeal expressed it thus,

> "In my view the judge was wrong to invoke the contra proferentem principle in this case. It is an approach to construction to which resort may properly be had when the language chosen by the parties is one-sided and genuinely ambiguous, that is, equally capable of bearing two distinct meanings. In such cases the application of the principle may enable the court to choose the meaning that is less favourable to the party who introduced the clause or in whose favour it operates. ... It has no part to play, however, when the meaning of the words is clear, as I think they are in this case; nor does it have a role to play in relation to a clause which favours both parties equally, especially where they are of equal bargaining power. In the case of a mutual clause such as the present clause 20 it is impossible to say who is the proferens and who the proferee."

In other words, the principle of *contra proferentem* is still technically alive, but the circumstances in which it may be successfully invoked are now small – really just the cases mentioned by Moore-Bick LJ above. The mention in that quotation of "equal bargaining power" also raises the prospect of a court relying on the principle where there is a genuine imbalance of commercial power and one party has been more or less forced to accept a disadvantageous liability provision or an indemnity.

This same approach to ousting the role of *contra proferentem* can be illustrated in the insurance arena by the recent case of *Spire Healthcare v Royal & Sun Alliance Insurance* [2018] EWCA Civ 317. The case revolved around the correct construction of what was said to be an aggregation clause but the Court of Appeal had no doubt that the principle of *contra proferentem* could only apply in cases of actual ambiguity, not as a general approach to cutting down the scope of the indemnity. They quoted from another recent case at Court of Appeal level on the same subject in the context of insurance, namely, *Impact Funding Solutions v Barrington Services* [2017] AC 73 where the Court of Appeal had said,

> "*As I see no ambiguity in the way that the Policy defined its cover and as the exclusion clause reflected what The Law Society of England and Wales as the regulator of the solicitors' profession had authorised as a limitation of professional indemnity cover, I see no role in this case for the doctrine of interpretation contra proferentem. ...*"

There is no reason why cases in the field of insurance when relating to a contract of indemnity insurance should not be equally applicable to a contractual indemnity in the non-insurance field, and this indeed appears to be the case as can be seen from *Transocean*.

Fault and indemnities

Only a few years ago, this section might have merited an extensive discussion covering many cases going back over several decades but, for reasons about to be made clear, this is (possibly or even probably) no longer so. The question is whether an indemnifier is to be taken as indemnifying the indemnified even against the consequences of the latter's own fault (or negligence). In a sense, it is the corollary of the principle of *contra proferentem*, the idea that an indemnity should be restrictively construed to benefit the indemnifier.

The need for the discussion derives from *Canada Steamship v The King* [1952] AC 192[12] where the Crown leased a shed to a shipping company. Clause 7 of the contract provided that the lessee would not have any claim against the Crown for damage to the shed or to any goods placed in it. Clause 17 went on to provide a comprehensive indemnity in favour of the Crown,

> *"... the lessee shall at all times indemnify ... the lessor ... against all claims and demands, loss, costs, damages, actions, suits or other proceedings by whomsoever made, brought or prosecuted, in any manner based upon, occasioned by or attributable to the execution of these presents, or any action taken or things done or maintained by virtue hereof, or the exercise in any manner of rights arising hereunder."*

The Crown's employees were undertaking repairs to the shed during which the shed and its contents were burnt down and destroyed. The

---

[12] This case developed from earlier authority including the well known case of *Alderslade v Hendon Laundry Ltd* [1945] K.B. 189

lessee sued the Crown for the latter's negligence and was met with the Crown's reliance on the two clauses just stated. One question which ultimately went to the Privy Council was whether the indemnity should be read as including an obligation to indemnify the Crown against the consequences of its own negligence.

We will look at the three "rules" propounded by the Privy Council presently, but for present purposes it suffices to say that the Crown was found to be unable to rely on these clauses as a defence to its own negligence. The court put forward three "rules" or approaches to construction that applied equally to liability clauses as much as to indemnities. It is worth noting that the *Canada Steamship* case is the reason why lawyers always use the formula "tort (including negligence)" when drafting liability provisions. The practice stems from this case which decided in effect that liability for negligence is not excluded unless it is specifically referred to. Whether this is strictly necessary now is open to question in the light of more recent authorities which rely on the modern approach to construction described above[13].

Along with *contra proferentem*, this principle in *Canada Steamship* has not fared well in recent years with the courts taking a much more literalistic approach to construction as has been noted above. In *Greenwich Millennium v Essex Services* [2014] EWCA Civ 960, when considering the construction of an indemnity, Jackson LJ said in the Court of Appeal,

> "*In my view the rule of construction stated in Canada Steamship … is of general application. Nevertheless it is based*

---

[13] Clearly, prudence would suggest maintaining the current practice to avoid any possible doubt on the matter.

upon the presumed intention of the parties. In applying that rule the court must have regard to the commercial context of the contract under consideration. In the case of a construction contract a failure by the indemnitee to spot defects perpetrated by its contractor or sub-contractor should not ordinarily defeat the operation of an indemnity clause, even if that clause fails expressly to encompass damage caused by the negligence of the indemnitee."

Just three years later, the same judge in the Court of Appeal in *Persimmon Homes v Ove Arup* [2017] EWCA Civ 373 said when dealing with an exclusion of liability,

"In recent years, and especially since the enactment of UCTA, the courts have softened their approach to both indemnity clauses and exemption clauses: see Lictor Anstalt v MIR Steel UK [2012] EWCA Civ 1397 ... at [31] to [34]. Although the present judgment is not the place for a general review of the law of contract, my impression is that, at any rate in commercial contracts, the Canada Steamship guidelines (in so far as they survive) are now more relevant to indemnity clauses than to exemption clauses."

While it can be seen that the court is leaving the door open to an argument based on an application of the "rules" in *Canada Steamship*, neither of these *dicta* is exactly a ringing endorsement of the principles contained in that case.

The important point to make at this stage is that the drafter of an indemnity clause should be aware of the *Canada Steamship* "rules" and be prepared to deal with the issue of fault in the indemnity clause itself.

If that same drafter fails to deal with the issue, then he should be prepared to anticipate uncertainty in the application of the clause as it may leave the clause open to arguments about whether or not *Canada Steamship* still applies in the modern law and, if it does, what the effect of the three "rules" is in the operation of the indemnity clause.

With that said, let us turn to look at the three "rules" and how the courts have applied them in the context of indemnities. "Rules" has been put in inverted commas, as they are not strictly speaking rules, rather three approaches to construction. As Jackson LJ observed in *Greenwich Millennium* quoted above, they are based on the presumed intention of the parties. By the time the same judge gave judgment in *Persimmon Homes*, it will be seen that he used the word "guidelines" and that expression is probably better as a description despite courts over the years using the word "rules". They are guidelines, or approaches to construction, not invariable rules. They are based on the presumption that an indemnifier in a regular commercial contract is unlikely to have intended to indemnify the indemnified against his own negligence. As with *contra proferentem*, if the words on the page actually say that, then the court will likely apply those words following the modern more literalistic approach to construction.

When looking at the three "rules" (or "guidelines"), it should be recalled that they were originally expressed to deal with both liability clauses and indemnities although, as has been pointed out above, they probably have even less significance – if indeed they have any significance – when talking about liabilities these days.

Canada Steamship – the first "rule"

This states that effect will not be given to an indemnity so as to protect an indemnified against the consequences of its own negligence unless it contains express language to that effect.

Despite the inflexible appearance of this "rule", the courts have in various cases found that the presence of the word "negligence" is not absolutely crucial and an equivalent can be used instead if the meaning is clear. In *Gillespie Brothers v Roy Bowles Transport* [1973] QB 400, when dealing with an indemnity against *"all claims or demands whatsoever"*, the Court of Appeal thought that it was sufficient to encompass negligence as a consequence of using the word "whatsoever".

We have already seen another example of clear wording sufficient to include negligence in the case of *Arthur White v Tarmac* [1967] 1 WLR 1508, where Arthur White had hired a digger and driver to Tarmac. The digger driver's negligence caused serious injuries to a third party for which the court found both Arthur White and Tarmac liable for breach of statutory duty. It will be recalled that this case was a "quasi-indemnity" in that the relevant provision did not use the word "indemnity",

> *"Handling of Plant. 8. When a driver or operator is supplied by [Whites] to work the plant, he shall be under the direction and control of [Tarmac]. Such drivers or operators shall for all purposes in connection with their employment in the working of the plant be regarded as the servants or agents of [Tarmac] who alone shall be responsible for all claims arising in connection with the operation of the plant by the said drivers or operators."*

The House of Lords found that the wording was clear enough to make it clear that the driver was to be regarded as Tarmac's employee for all purposes and that the wording covered everything, effectively transferring total responsibility to Tarmac. It was irrelevant that the digger was actually idle at the time of the accident and not engaged in any active work on the site[14].

Canada Steamship – the second "rule"

This states that, without an express reference to negligence, the court will consider whether the words are sufficiently wide in their ordinary meaning to cover negligence, with any doubt being resolved in favour of the indemnifier.

It is at this point that the *Canada Steamship* "rules" approach most closely to the principle of *contra proferentem*. This rule reflects an interventionist approach by the courts which scrutinised liability and indemnity clauses to seek to ensure fair play as between the parties. As has been pointed out in more than one judgment in recent years, that role is less important now in the light of the Unfair Contract Terms Act 1977 and its (albeit limited) role in regulating the terms of commercial contracts.

The case of *Smith v South Wales Switchgear* [1978] 1 WLR 165 is often taken as being the high water mark of the application of the second "rule". Switchgear had been retained by Chrysler to overhaul electrical equipment at its factory in Scotland. One Smith was employed by

---

[14] In this sense, the result in this case can be compared with the Canadian case of *Salmon River Logging v Burt Bros.* [1953] 2 SCR 117, the first case considered in this book: the court there applied both *contra proferentem* and *Canada Steamship* to reach the opposite conclusion.

Switchgear and became injured as a result of Chrysler's negligence and breach of statutory duty. The contract between Chrysler and Switchgear provided,

> *"[Switchgear] will keep [Chrysler] indemnified against: ... (b) Any liability, loss, claim or proceedings whatsoever under statute or common law (i) in respect of personal injury ... "*

The House of Lords applied the second "rule" finding that it made commercial sense to apply an indemnity for the negligence of Switchgear's staff working on Chrysler's premises. However, in the court's view, there was no reason to suppose that the indemnity should go further and be held to apply to the negligence of Chrysler's employees and they were not prepared to construe the indemnity in that way.

Canada Steamship – the third "rule"

This states that an indemnity will not include the consequences of the indemnified's negligence if you can find another cause of action not based on negligence, so long as it is not fanciful or remote.

The courts have a natural reluctance to accept that one party to a commercial contract has undertaken effectively to insure the other. An interesting example of the application of this third "rule" can be found in *Jose v MacSalvors Plant Hire* [2009] EWCA Civ 1329. Brush Transformers was carrying out work on an electricity substation. They hired a crane and operator from MacSalvors. Jose was the driver employed by MacSalvors and was operating the crane on site. After stepping out of his cab to carry out some routine maintenance duties, he fell off the platform and suffered injuries.

Jose claimed against MacSalvors, his employers, for his injuries and that claim was settled with Jose accepting that he had been 25% contributorily negligent. MacSalvors then claimed indemnity from Brush Transformers under the contract in place between them. The wording was almost identical to that in *Arthur White* considered above and read,

> *"8. HANDLING OF PLANT When a driver or operator ... is supplied by the Owner with the plant, ... such person shall be under the direction and control of the Hirer. Such drivers or operators or persons shall for all purposes in connection with their employment in the working of the plant be regarded as the servants or agents of the Hirer (but without prejudice to any of the provisions of Clause 13) who also shall be responsible for all claims arising in connection with the operation of the plant by the said drivers/operators/persons. ..."*

Even without the authority of *Arthur White,* which was not apparently cited to the court, the Court of Appeal read the clause as making Brush Transformers as hirer responsible for negligent operation of the crane leading to claims by third parties. What was not contemplated or included in the clause was making Brush Transformers (the hirer) responsible for a claim against MacSalvors (the owner) for MacSalvors' own negligence. The Court of Appeal therefore rejected the argument that "for all purposes" and "all claims" had such a wide meaning even though on their face they might bear that meaning.

This was the same conclusion as in *Arthur White,* and the court in that case did not go on to consider the indemnity in clause 13 which the court in *Jose* did. By clause 13, Brush Transformers as hirer must,

> *"fully and completely indemnify [MacSalvors] in respect of all claims by any person whatsoever for injury to person or property caused by or in connection with or arising out of the ... use of the plant during the continuance of the hire period ..."*

Again, the argument for MacSalvors was to the effect that this wording referred to "all claims" by "any person whatsoever", which they said was wide enough to include what had happened. The Court of Appeal disagreed, relying on an unreported decision by an earlier Court of Appeal considering words in the same contract[15]. In that earlier case, an excavator was hired out and was being driven on a loader along a motorway when it collided with a low bridge causing significant damage. Did those same words in clause 13 put an obligation on the hirer to indemnify the owner for its own negligence? The Court of Appeal considered the third "rule" in *Canada Steamship* and concluded that there were indeed a number of other possible heads that clause 13 was intended to address without concluding that it obliged the hirer to indemnify the owner for its own negligence. As Slade LJ put it,

> *"I reach this conclusion without great regret. I can well understand that the plaintiffs, and many other members of the Contractors Plant Association who use the C.P.A. conditions, would like to be in a position to invoke clause 13 in appropriate circumstances for the purpose of exempting themselves from loss caused by their own personal negligence and that of their servants, and even that of claiming an indemnity in respect of such loss. But it does not seem to me either inequitable or contrary to public policy to require contractors who intend to*

---

[15] *E. Scott (Plant Hire) Ltd v British Waterways Board*, 20th December 1982

> *demand such very extensive protection for themselves from their customers to bring their intentions to the notice of prospective hirers in the most specific terms – far clearer than those employed in the present case."*

The Court of Appeal in *Jose v MacSalvors Plant Hire* [2009] EWCA Civ 1329 decided that it was bound by this decision on the same wording and decided against MacSalvors (the owners).

It has been noted above that *Canada Steamship* has been slowly declining in importance over a number of years, certainly as regards liability provisions: while the unreported decision of the Court of Appeal in 1982 in *Scott v British Waterways Board* might still be thought to be in thrall to the judgment of the Privy Council in *Canada Steamship*, with an echo of that in 2009 when *Jose* was decided, it is submitted that modern courts would be more likely to approach the matter as purely one of construction rather than a process of applying fixed "rules" in sequence for determining the true meaning of an indemnity. That being so, a court approaching clause 13 today would probably come to the same conclusion, based on an approach that took account of the context and using that context to construe the words actually used. It would be unlikely that a hirer would effectively agree to step in and act as insurer for the owner of machinery so as to provide insurance cover for the owner's operations: unlikely – but not impossible if the words were really explicit.

The modern take on *Canada Steamship*

The above discussion appears to be the way that judges are nowadays construing indemnities in regard to fault on the part of the indemnified. This is illustrated by *Cape Distribution v Cape Intermediate Holdings* [2016] EWHC 1119 (QB). The case concerned the manufacture of asbestos and the consequent claims for compensation from employees and former employees. Cape Distribution (CDL) was the subsidiary of Cape Intermediate Holdings (CIH) which carried on this business but, in 1964, executed a sale agreement with CIH transferring its business to CIH. Clause 5 contained an indemnity clause as follows,

> *"Until the completion of the sale [CDL] shall carry on the business of [CDL] as heretofore and shall in so doing be deemed to be the agent of [CIH] and shall account and be entitled to be indemnified accordingly."*

Picken J paid scant consideration to *Canada Steamship* and simply described them as *"being a useful guide and not more than that"* before deciding that the very broad words of the indemnity were sufficient to include CDL's own negligence, taking into account the commercial context, namely, that the transaction was part of a wider settlement providing that CIH would henceforth be taking primary responsibility for the carrying out of CDL's business. It would not make commercial sense to carve out negligence in these circumstances.

The recent judgment of Foxton J in *CNM Estates v VeCREF I* [2020] EWHC 1605 (Comm) appeared on 22 June 2020. The court's treatment of the *Canada Steamship* principle largely bears out what has been written above although the judge entered into a detailed treatment of the *Canada Steamship* principles in contradistinction to the more superficial treatment given to these principles by other judges recently.

The case was a trial of various preliminary issues. It covered some of the classic problems with exemption clauses, and one issue given extensive consideration was the *Canada Steamship* case. CNM was a property developer which had entered into various financing contracts to secure money for the redevelopment of Tolworth Tower near Surbiton. The premises were part of the security provided in return for the money. Following a failure to make repayment, receivers were appointed. CNM's allegation was that the receivers had failed to get the best price available in the market on the sale of Tolworth Tower (what the judge referred to as the "Equitable Duty of Care").

The judge looked at clause 19.1 of the Debenture, which read,

> *"19 Liability of Security Agent and Receiver*
>
> *19.1 Liability*
>
> *Neither the Security Agent, any Receiver nor any of their respective Delegates and sub-delegates (whether as mortgagee in possession or otherwise) shall either by reason of:*
>
> > *(a) taking possession of or realising all or part of the Secured Assets; or*
> >
> > *(b) taking any action permitted by this Deed,*
>
> *be liable to a Chargor or any other person for any costs, losses or liabilities relating to any of the Secured Assets or for any act, default, omission or misconduct of the Security Agent, any Receiver or their respective Delegates and sub-delegates in relation to the Secured Assets or otherwise."*

The court considered the three principles derived from *Canada Steamship* (as well as a host of cases which had considered or applied that case) and concluded that these words of clause 19.1 did not exclude the receivers' liability for breach of the Equitable Duty of Care.

While the judge did run through the three principles of *Canada Steamship*, the case is remarkable for his reaching his conclusion through the application of ordinary principles of construction rather than a mechanistic application of "rules" mandated by the *Canada Steamship* case:

- The clause did not on its terms apply to a separate breach of duty, it referred in paragraph (b) to "taking any action permitted by this Deed", which rather left open a separate duty such as the Equitable Duty of Care

- Reading the clause in context, other provisions provided for the receivers to be liable for "gross negligence or wilful misconduct", so it was unlikely that this provision was intended to exclude all liability whatsoever

- There were other things that the clause was realistically intended to cover such as the receivers failing to hand over the proceeds of sale or rent, or their fiduciary duties

These points certainly do correspond to the three "rules" in *Canada Steamship* but the judge achieved the same result by applying ordinary rules of construction. The same point could be made concerning the court's consideration of the exemption clause contained in the Intercreditor Agreement. In conclusion, *Canada Steamship* is still there, still a lively doctrine and capable of being cited to the court, but the court is likely to apply modern rules of construction, using *Canada Steamship* simply as a test to ensure that a common sense result is achieved rather than a set of principles pointing towards, let alone mandating, a particular result.

Practice point

The drafting point coming out of these cases dealing with *Canada Steamship* and their somewhat dubious status in the modern law is to ensure that drafting of an indemnity is clear on the question of fault, in particular on the question of whether one party is expected to stand in to act as insurer for the other party's own negligence.

Equally, whenever the reviewer of a contract sees an indemnity, it is necessary to step back and ask whether it is intended to apply to the fault of either party, or just to the fault of one. As always with indemnities, it comes down to clarity of wording.

A recent example of fault and indemnities

The case of *Greenwich Millennium Village v Essex Services* [2014] EWCA Civ 960 provides a good example of how a modern court is likely to approach the question of fault in indemnity clauses. Robson supplied labour to provide the plumbing on the construction of two blocks of flats. In the contract chain, it was the sub-sub-sub-contractor to HSE Environmental Services. In the contract between Robson and HSE, it provided,

> *"[Robson] hereby agrees ... further to indemnify [HSE] in respect of any liability, loss, claim or proceedings of whatsoever nature such as shall arise by virtue of the breach or breaches of this Subcontract Agreement by, or act, default or negligence of [Robson]."*

The labour provided by Robson performed their work defectively and the consequence was serious flooding of the blocks of flats and substantial damage. Robson could not deny that its workmanship was defective on the facts but did argue that HSE was also at fault in that it was evident on handover that the work was in a defective state. HSE had inspected the work and accepted it, while photographs retained showed that the workmanship was obviously defective. The argument was to the effect that, given that the defects were patent and not hidden, HSE's failure to notice them meant that the subsequent flooding was attributable, not to Robson, but to HSE's own fault.

The Court of Appeal rejected the argument that HSE was thereby unable to claim under the indemnity. The Court of Appeal simply applied the words of the indemnity. As Jackson LJ put it,

> *"Despite the rule of construction formulated in Canada Steamship and Walters v Whessoe, it cannot be presumed that the parties intended to confine [the indemnity] to workmanship breaches by this labour only sub-sub-sub-contractor which were invisible upon reasonable inspection. The clause does not say that. No-one other than an enthusiastic reader of the law reports would think of construing it in that way."*

As can be seen from this whole discussion on fault, the arguments are still technically lively in that arguments based on *Canada Steamship* and the others continue to be made. The reality is that modern courts tend to downplay them and look to the specific wording of the indemnity rather than apply it in accordance with a set of predetermined "rules" or assumptions about what the parties wanted to achieve by their indemnity.

What is "fault"?

We have been proceeding so far on the assumption, by and large, that fault equates to negligence, the tort at common law. There are other, similar bases of liability, not least breach of statutory duty, which may or may not overlap with common law negligence. Breach of statutory duty may not involve "fault" as it may depend on strict liability. The tort of negligence may or may not overlap with the breach of a contractual duty to take reasonable care. How does this impact an indemnity provision?

The point came up in *EE Caledonia v Orbit Valve* [1994] 1 WLR 1515. This was one of many cases arising out of the 1988 Piper Alpha explosion and fire that claimed so many lives and caused so many injuries. One Quinn had been employed by Orbit, which had supplied Caledonia with certain valves and now contracted to provide the services of Quinn to overhaul them. Quinn was one of the first to die from asphyxiation after the explosion but his work had had no role whatsoever in the explosion or subsequent fire.

Caledonia's liability for the explosion was agreed to be concurrent, that is, arising out of the negligence of one of Caledonia's employees and also out of various breaches of statutory duty. The claim brought by Quinn's estate was settled and Caledonia brought a claim under the indemnity contained in the agreement with Orbit.

The indemnity in question was complex and its relevant part, clause 10(b), read,

> *"(b) Company's and contractor's employees and property. Each party hereto shall indemnify, defend and hold harmless the other, provided that the other party has acted in good faith, from and against any claim, demand, cause of action, loss, expense or*

liability (including the cost of litigation) arising by reason of any injury to or death of an employee, or damage, loss or destruction of any property, of the indemnifying party, resulting from or in any way connected with the performance of this order."

It is obviously a reciprocal indemnity but does not mention negligence or even equivalent words having that meaning; to be fair, it does not mention breach of statutory duty either. Aid was sought from *Canada Steamship* and, in particular, the third principle – was there some other principle other than negligence that the clause could cover, so long as it was not fanciful or remote? In the view of the judge and of the Court of Appeal, the wording of the indemnity was not apt to include negligence. For Steyn LJ, the "man on the Clapham omnibus" was replaced by the "draftsman on the underground": that lawyer would well understand why reference to negligence was omitted. It was a deliberate omission so that one or other of the parties would not be frightened off while reading it.

The difficulty is that Caledonia caused the explosion by the negligence of one of its employees, which also happened to be in breach of various statutory duties. If the indemnity did not apply to negligence, could recovery nonetheless be allowed for breach of statutory duty? The approach of the Court of Appeal was to see clause 10(b) as an allocation of risk, meaning that each party assumed the risk of its own negligence. That being so, where there were concurrent causes of action, one being negligence and the other some other ground, clause 10(b) should be construed so as not to allow recovery. Given that the clause did not apply to negligence, it would be surprising, so reasoned the Court of Appeal, if the indemnity allowed recovery under some other ground. The fact of negligence extinguished, as it were, other possible grounds of recovery.

Like all cases on indemnities, the case is an interesting application of the law as applied to one particular provision, and a baffling provision at that. The real problem was that the lawyers responsible for drafting the clause in the first place had completely omitted to specify the precise grounds for making a claim under the indemnity clause: did it cover negligence, breach of contract, breach of a contractual duty to take reasonable care, breach of statutory duty or some other ground? Given the oddity of the wording, this case is probably confined to its own facts and should be compared with *Murfin v United Steel* [1957] 1 WLR 104, considered in the next section.

Some final thoughts on fault and indemnities

We have engaged in some discussion of fault and of negligence in particular. However, when drafting an indemnity, regard should be given to the various ways in which "fault" can occur: it may be in the context of the tort of negligence, a contractual duty to take reasonable care or breach of statutory duty (the last of which may not include any "fault" at all in the moral sense as the relevant statute imposes a strict liability).

The case normally referred to on the question of breach of statutory duty is *Murfin v United Steel* [1957] 1 WLR 104. Murfin was an employee of contractors working on electrical equipment operated by United Steel at their premises. Murfin was detailed to replace a burnt out overload trip unit but there was no screening of surrounding live panels. Murfin fell onto a live panel and was electrocuted to death. The claim was brought by his widow and administratrix.

It was found that United Steel was not liable in negligence, but was liable for breach of statutory duty in failing to have the live parts screened. The contract between United Steel and Murfin's employer provided for an indemnity by the latter in favour of United Steel in respect of claims,

> *"When work is carried out on ... the company's premises ... the contractor shall be liable for and shall indemnify the company against every claim against the company under any statute or at common law for ... (b) death ... arising out of or in connexion with the carrying out of the contractor's work and from any cause other than the negligence of the company or its employee."*

United Steel claimed indemnity from Murfin's employer pursuant to this indemnity. The question was whether the word "negligence" appearing at the end of the clause of itself included breach of statutory duty. Construing the words themselves, they opened by referring to both statute and common law, and so were apt to include either a claim in negligence or statutory duty. However, the exception wording which followed immediately referred only to negligence. In the view of the Court of Appeal, that difference was deliberate, and was designed to ensure that the indemnity only operated where there was a breach of statutory duty in the absence of negligence: indeed, if "negligence" in the closing exceptions wording included both common law negligence and breach of statutory duty, then the indemnity would seldom operate as the exceptions wording would work to defeat the vast majority of claims by the indemnified.

Again, the drafting point coming out of this is clear: when thinking about fault or negligence in general, it is necessary to be precise as to what is comprehended within the term: as seen above, "fault" could comprehend the tort of negligence, a failure to exercise a contractual duty to take reasonable care, breach of statutory duty as well as perhaps other grounds of liability besides.

Legal costs

An indemnity will frequently cover the indemnified's legal costs and these are often expressed to be "reasonable" legal costs. What are "reasonable" legal costs? There is a relatively little consistent authority for what is nowadays a ubiquitous expression: it is another area perhaps where commercial lawyers who have become so fond of including indemnities in respect of "reasonable legal costs" are perhaps unaware of just how little consistent authority there is out there on what the words actually mean.

First, let us look at an older authority. In *Maxwell v British Thomson Houston* [1904] 2 KB 342 (KB) Maxwell sued British for injuries caused to her by a subcontractor of British, which had left a metal rod overhanging a tramway, which struck Maxwell as she travelled on the top of the tram. The subcontract contained an indemnity from the subcontractor in favour of British to be answerable for all accidents and damages personal, consequential, or otherwise that might occur during the progress of the work, and to indemnify and bear British harmless therefrom. British lost the case and appealed, giving notice to the subcontractor, which decided to take no active part in the proceedings. British lost on appeal but then sought to recover the total legal costs from the subcontractor under the indemnity. It was held that, in the absence of special circumstances, the costs of an appeal from an unsuccessful judgment would not be recoverable. Kennedy J also thought that any legal costs recovered would be on a party and party basis, not solicitor and own client.

A more modern approach can be seen in *Alafco Irish Leasing v Hong Kong Airlines* [2019] EWHC 3668 (Comm). Alafco had sued Hong Kong to recover lease payments. Clause 25.4.2 of the lease provided,

> *"[Hong Kong] shall pay to [Alafco] on demand all reasonable costs and expenses (including reasonable legal expenses) incurred by [Alafco] ... in connection with any amendment to, or the granting of any waiver or consent or the preservation of any rights of [Alafco] under, any [the lease] required in writing by [Hong Kong]."*

As we have seen already, the inclusion of "on demand" arguably means that this is not really an indemnity at all, but the court appears to have proceeded on the basis that it was. The court accepted that the clause, properly construed, meant that Hong Kong had agreed to pay all reasonable costs and expenses including the costs of any litigation. The inclusion of "reasonable" did not mean that costs should not be paid on an indemnity basis. To come to this conclusion, the judge did consider two other recent cases, one which contained the word "reasonable" and the other which did not.

In *Littlestone v Macleish* [2016] EWCA Civ 127 the issue arose as to costs following an action for breach of a repairing obligation. The lease provided that the lessee would pay *"all costs and expenses (including legal costs and fees payable to a surveyor) which may be incurred by the Lessor"* in the recovering rent arrears. The Court of Appeal held that this meant an assessment on the indemnity, not the standard, basis: the reference to *"all costs and expenses"* was an indicator that no retrospective assessment of the costs would be undertaken, as might be the case in litigation when assessing costs on the standard basis.

It should be noted that there is another authority, *Euro-Asian Oil v Crédit Suisse* [2017] EWHC B7 (Comm) which distinguished *Littlestone*. The case concerned a claim for payment for diesel oil under a sale contract and related letter of indemnity. Euro-Asian was successful in obtaining judgment. In the subsequent costs hearing, Euro-Asian claimed its costs on an indemnity basis based on the wording in the letter of indemnity, which read in its relevant part,

> *"To protect, indemnify and to hold [Euro-Asia] harmless from and against any and all damages, costs and expenses (including reasonable attorney fees) which [Euro-Asia] may suffer by reason of the shipping documents, including the original clean and negotiable bills of lading remaining outstanding or by reason of a breach of the warranties given."*

For Cranston J in this case, the crucial distinction between this case and *Littlestone* was the presence of the word "reasonable" and indemnity costs could not be regarded as "reasonable". This left Euro-Asia entitled to costs on the standard basis, which was no better than what it was entitled to according to ordinary principles.

Practice point

The point is really a simple one: all indemnities come down at the end of the day to points of construction. While there is some guidance to be sought in the cases on the question of legal costs, it is not always possible to extract a consistent thread. Exactly this point can be seen in these few cases, one old and three new, which have taken divergent views on what legal fees can be recovered under an indemnity.

- When indemnifying a party against its legal fees, the inclusion of "reasonable" may or may not limit recovery to legal fees on the standard basis

- The really important point is that the contract should state what is intended

    o "Reasonable" could mean that an assessment is made of whether legal fees were reasonably incurred, after which they are paid on the indemnity basis

    o Alternatively, "reasonable" could mean that all legal fees are payable but only on the standard, not the indemnity, basis (to use the language of litigation)

    o If you refer to "all" legal fees without "reasonable", this might indicate an indemnity basis

There are possibly other possible permutations. When drafting "reasonable legal fees" (or equivalent words), try to set out what exactly is meant.

CHAPTER THREE
RECOVERING UNDER
AN INDEMNITY

"... A contract of insurance is a type of contract of indemnity characterised by the obligation to indemnify arising upon the happening of an event which is a risk. ..."[16]

This chapter will look at what it is necessary to show in order to recover under the indemnity. Many indemnities require some sort of notice to be given and to allow the indemnifier to take sole control of the defence of the action. Just as importantly, what exactly must the indemnified show in order to gain the benefit of the indemnity? What will that benefit be? This Chapter and the next on scope will look at these and related questions.

The "ticket to ride": notification as a condition precedent to recovering under an indemnity

Many, but not necessarily all, indemnity provisions will set out some sort of notification provision, obliging the indemnified to notify the indemnifier that e.g. a third party claim has been made which is said to

---

[16] *Durley House v Firmdale Hotels* [2014] EWHC 2608 (Ch) *per* Stephen Morris QC, sitting as a Deputy High Court judge.

be within the scope of the indemnity. The question then arises: what if notice is not given?

This came up in *Heritage Oil & Gas v Tullow Uganda* [2014] EWCA Civ 1048. There was an agreement by which Heritage sold its interests in various petroleum exploration areas in Uganda to Tullow. The Ugandan tax authorities believed Heritage was liable for sales tax on the profits, but Heritage disputed this. Heritage was by this stage non-resident in Uganda, so the tax authorities imposed the tax on the purchaser, Tullow (as they were lawfully entitled to do under Ugandan law). The facts were complex and the full history long drawn-out, but the Ugandan tax authorities communicated with both Heritage and Tullow over the course of some months in order to secure payment of the tax due.

In the sale agreement, it provided,

> *"7.5 Upon the Indemnified Party becoming aware of any Tax Claim being made to which the indemnities ... may apply, that Indemnified Party shall;*
>
> > *(a) within 20 (twenty) Business Days, give notice in writing of the Tax Claim to the Indemnifying Party; ..."*

While both parties were in communication with the Ugandan tax authorities and with each other, there was no formal notice given in accordance with this provision. Tullow had to take a decision as, without the Ugandan Government's permission, it could not operate the exploration areas it had purchased. Accordingly, it paid the tax demanded and sought to recover the same under the tax indemnity contained in the agreement. Heritage met this with the defence that no notice had been given under clause 7.5 and that, in consequence, the indemnity was not operative.

The Court of Appeal held that the requirement of notice was not a condition precedent to recovery under the indemnity clause. Clear words were required, in their view, before a requirement of notice became a condition precedent: it was not necessary to use the expression, "condition precedent" but either it or something equivalent had to be used. It was, thought the Court of Appeal, akin to the situation in insurance law: courts are normally reluctant to classify a notification of loss provision as a condition precedent, normally finding that there has to be some link between the obligation to give notice and the obligation to pay the claim.

A more recent example of the same principle in operation can be seen in *Gwynt Y Môr v Gwynt Y Môr Offshore Wind Farm* [2020] EWHC 850 (Comm) concerning the indemnity given on the sale of a business for the maintenance and operation of electrical transmission links. Clause 8.3 provided,

> *"If the [claimant] becomes aware of any Pre-Completion Damage which may give rise to a Claim the [claimant] shall:*
>
> > *8.3.1 give written notice (including reasonable particulars of such Third Party Claim or circumstance) to the Operating Company on behalf of the Vendors; ..."*

There then followed a detailed process for allowing the vendor to access the asset and for a proposal for repair or replacement to be agreed, failing which there was provision for resolution of the matter by an expert. Two underwater cables in fact failed due to corrosion consequent on seawater having entered the cables. The claimant saw to the repairs as a matter of urgency and claimed under the indemnity for the value of the repairs. However, it was about a year before written notice was given to the defendants, by which time the repairs had been carried out.

Philipps LJ decided that the clause did not create a condition precedent of notification such that notification was necessary before the indemnity could be relied on. Following the decision of Flaux J in *AstraZeneca v Albemarle International* [2011] EWHC 1574 (Comm), he held that the use of the expression "condition precedent" (or equivalent) was not essential, but without some such words, a condition precedent could only be found where one obligation clearly had to be performed first before another one could arise, or where actual performance of the first obligation was necessary to earn entitlement to the second. In this case, urgent repairs might be required to the assets being sold, making the process of notification and agreement of a remedy with a possible reference to an independent expert not only unnecessary, but actually inconvenient. There was no point imposing a requirement of prior notification where the claimant had already executed the repairs.

An even more recent example is the case of *Towergate Financial v Hopkinson* [2020] EWHC 984 (Comm). There was an SPA in August 2008 whereby Hopkinson (and others) sold shares in M2 Holdings Limited to Towergate Financial. Following reviews by the FCA into possible mis-selling of investments by M2 over the whole period from December 2001 to January 2014, substantial compensation was found to be owing to individuals for the historic mis-selling, the first such payment being made in January 2016. The SPA contained an indemnity clause in favour of Towergate Financial, but the clause in dispute was the notice of claims provision, clause 6.7:

"6.7 The Purchaser shall not make any Claims against the Warrantors nor shall the Warrantors have any liability in respect of any matter or thing unless notice in writing of the relevant matter or thing (specifying the details and circumstances giving rise to the Claim or Claims and an estimate in good faith of the total amount of such Claim or Claims) is given to all the Warrantors as soon as possible and in any event prior to:

> *6.7.1 the seventh anniversary of the date of this Agreement in the case of any Claim solely in relation to the Taxation Covenant;*
>
> *6.7.2 the date two years from the Completion Date in the case of any other Claim; and*
>
> *6.7.3 in relation to a claim under the indemnity in clause 5.9 on or before the seventh anniversary of the date of this Agreement."*

A point that is made several times in this book is that some cases, this being one of them, should serve as a warning to those who say that an indemnity makes recovery easy: this case had already been to the High Court and on appeal to the Court of Appeal on related issues of construction (*Towergate Financial Group v Clark* [2017] EWHC 2330 (Comm) and *Hopkinson & Ors v Towergate Financial (Group) Ltd & Ors* [2018] EWCA Civ 2744). Including an indemnity in your contract is not necessarily a means of securing quick compensation.

While at first sight clause 6.7 might look straightforward, it is shot through with uncertainties, not least the presence of references to a "Claim" (note the capital 'C') and the single reference to a "claim" (note the small 'c') in clause 6.7.3 when dealing with the indemnity. Consequent on the decision of the Court of Appeal on the applicability of the wording specific to the indemnity in clause 6.7.3 as opposed to the other "Claims", which were defined terms dealing with different, non-indemnity, claims, the judge in this case found that the clause, insofar as it related to the indemnity, should be read,

> "~~The Purchaser shall not make any Claims against the Warrantors~~ nor shall ~~the~~ [such of the Warrantors as have given the indemnity under clause 5.9] have any liability in respect of any matter or thing unless notice in writing of the relevant matter or thing ~~(specifying the details and circumstances giving rise to the Claim or Claims and an estimate in good faith of the total amount of such Claim or Claims)~~ is given to all the Warrantors as soon as possible and in any event prior to:

>> ~~6.7.1 the seventh anniversary of the date of this Agreement in the case of any Claim solely in relation to the Taxation Covenant;~~

>> ~~6.7.2 the date two years from the Completion Date in the case of any other Claim; and~~

>> 6.7.3 in relation to a claim under the indemnity in clause 5.9 on or before the seventh anniversary of the date of this Agreement."

One of the questions for the judge was the meaning of "as soon as possible and in event prior to" in the introductory wording: did this create two conditions precedent, or in reality was there just the one condition precedent, namely, the seven year longstop date for bringing indemnity claims as set out in clause 6.7.3?

After taking into account both textual and contextual considerations, Cockerill J held that there were in reality two conditions precedent: there was indeed a seven year longstop date for serving notice, but she upheld the wording "as soon as possible" as being sufficiently clear to act as a separate condition precedent for recovery under the indemnity clause. The notice had been served just before the expiry of the seven year date: this was held insufficient, as by then Towergate Financial had long since involved its own insurers and had made substantial payments of compensation to disappointed investors.

Practice point

There is no fixed "law" determining whether a notification of claim provision coupled with an indemnity is always to be read as a condition precedent, rather, the cases give an indication of the way courts will approach the provision in question. In reality, it comes down to the specific words used coupled with the admissible context: as the Court of Appeal observed in *Heritage Oil and Gas v Tullow Uganda* [2014] EWCA Civ 1048, there was *"some reluctance to classify notification of loss provisions as conditions precedent"* (paragraph 34).

While there is no presumption that a notification provision is not a condition precedent to recovery under an indemnity, it does seem clear that the courts will approach these provisions with a cautious mindset, not being too hasty to find a condition precedent.

That being so, for drafting purposes, care should be taken in drafting a notification provision: if it is intended that notification should be a true condition precedent to recovery under the indemnity, that needs to be expressly stated – not, indeed, having to use the formal expression "condition precedent" (thought it would do no harm to do so), but using words having that effect.

Liability or expense actually incurred: when does the indemnity bite?

A little appreciated feature of indemnities is that the indemnity is, in general, only engaged when there is an established liability. As will be seen, this is not an inevitable conclusion, however. Therefore, if an indemnity is given to the indemnified against third party claims, there must in general be a liability to the third party first before the liability to indemnify arises. Everything will depend on the precise wording of the indemnity.

For example, in *Bradford v Gammon* [1925] Ch 132, a partnership deed provided for the sale of a certain plot of land. It further provided that, if one partner should die, the others would buy his share and indemnify the dead partner's personal representatives against future claims, liabilities and demands.

One partner did in fact die and there was bank overdraft in favour of the partners at the time of around £17,000. The plaintiff was the dead partner's personal representative who commenced proceedings for a declaration that the indemnities were activated such that the remaining partners should pay off the overdraft at the bank. All that had in fact happened was that the bank had closed the account on being told of the partner's death, had assessed the amount owing and told the surviving partners of this.

The claim failed: there was no existing liability as such in the absence of a demand. As Eve J put it,

> *"So long as the covenantee is kept indemnified he cannot in my opinion insist on the covenantor discharging debts for which no demand has been made; the obligation is to make good the indemnity by paying and the right to enforce the covenant arises when the demand is made and not before. I think the plaintiff's claim fails, ..."*

It is not really a matter of principle, rather a question of construction. In *K/S Preston Street v Santander* [2012] EWHC 1633 (Ch), Preston Street had borrowed a maximum of £2.26 million under the terms of a facility agreement. It made early repayment and Santander claimed losses arising from the "prepayment", which Preston Street disputed. The relevant indemnity read as follows,

> *"In addition to any prepayment costs payable under para.9, the partnership shall indemnify the bank on demand against any cost, loss, expenses or liability (including loss of profit and opportunity costs) which the bank incurs as a result of the repayment of the loan during the fixed rate period or any further period during which the rate of interest applicable to the loan is fixed."*

Paragraph 9 set out a sliding scale of fees for early repayment: in year six, when Preston Street made early repayment, no fees were payable. Santander claimed just over £170,000 by way of compensation for loss of income/profit and loss of opportunity. But just when did the indemnity bite?

HH Judge Pelling QC examined the wording and thought that the use of "indemnify" must have meant there had to be some sort of crystallised liability or obligation – that any "cost, loss, expense or liability" had actually to have been incurred. The clause read, "which the bank incurs" – not "... incurs or to be incurred". Again, the judge thought that including "on demand" meant that it could not refer to a loss that had not yet been incurred. The result was that the judgment could only be made in Santander's favour to the extent of losses actually incurred at the time of its demand (or possibly when the claim form was issued or even later). This was not of course what was claimed by Santander, which had produced a calculation showing by and large its future losses resulting from "prepayment" of the facility.

A more recent example can be seen in *Minera Las Bambas v Glencore* [2019] EWCA Civ 972. Glencore sold the shares in a Peruvian mining company to Minera, part of the deal being that Minera would re-settle a local population to a new town, yet to be built. The Peruvian tax authorities, known as the SUNAT, investigated the matter to ascertain whether any VAT was payable on various parts of the transaction. After considering the matter, it issued a formal assessment for VAT it said was due. After hearing an appeal against the assessment, it issued a further assessment, confirming that VAT was indeed due. The original share purchase agreement contained general indemnities, and the parties also entered into a further tax indemnity deed.

The share purchase agreement provided,

> *"Glencore] shall indemnify [Minera] in relation to, and covenant to pay [Minera] an amount equal to:*

10.1.1 the amount of any Tax payable by [[Minera]] to the extent the Tax has not been discharged or paid on or prior to the Effective Time and it:

(i) relates to any period, or part period, up to and including Closing;"

The tax indemnity deed provided for Glencore,

"to indemnify [[Minera]] against the full amount (if any) payable by [[Minera]] under each of the Assumed Tax Matters (if adversely determined)."

In both cases, the indemnity would bite when the tax was "payable", but the question then arose when this would be. There are various candidates for the meaning of this expression, including

- Following an assessment by SUNAT

- Following the assessment by SUNAT after an appeal

- Following a judgment of the Peruvian courts confirming the assessment

In fact, there was an appeal still outstanding to the Peruvian courts at the time of hearing the appeal in this case. The question was important since the SUNAT operated, along with many other tax authorities, a "graduality" regime i.e. penalties and interest on penalties were lower the sooner the taxpayer paid the tax. There was thus an incentive to pay the tax early, but Minera was reluctant to do so unless it was put in funds first by Glencore. So the question of when the indemnity actually operated had to be decided.

The trial judge, after hearing evidence on the matter, held that payment of the tax assessed by SUNAT would not become "coercively enforceable" until there was a judgment of the Peruvian courts. In other words, the SUNAT's assessment of tax due was precisely that – an assessment, but the SUNAT could do nothing to recover it unless and until the Peruvian courts had upheld its assessment.

The Court of Appeal agreed with the trial judge and held that "payable" meant following a decision by the Peruvian courts. In other words, Minera could pay early to avoid penalties and interest, but it could not reclaim the money under the indemnity from Glencore until the Peruvian courts had upheld the assessment.

Again, the use of words without thought for their consequences can lead to disputes. A recent example is *AXA v Genworth Financial* [2020] EWHC 2024 (Comm): we have already reviewed this case when we looked at its first outing to the High Court on the question of liability ([2019] EWHC 3376 (Comm)). We saw that Genworth had agreed to pay "on demand" 90% of certain PPI mis-selling losses on the sale of two subsidiaries to AXA. Those two subsidiaries had been active in underwriting PPI and the parties were well aware of the possibility of large liabilities attaching to their past activities – just how large those liabilities turned out to be was probably not appreciated by either party at the time as, by the time of the hearing on quantum, the amount was nearly £500m.

The obligation in clause 10.8 of the SPA was to pay 90% of *"Relevant Distributor Mis-selling Losses"* and 90% of the amount of *"all costs, claims, damages, expenses or any other losses incurred by [AXA] ...".* *"Relevant Distributor Mis-selling Losses"* was defined and the definition in turn referred out to *"PPI Mis-selling Losses"* which was in turn defined to mean *"all damages, losses, liabilities, penalties, fines, costs, interest and expenses ... incurred by [AXA]"*. One irony is that, out of the plethora of defined terms, the word "incurred" occurs twice in the quoted text above but did not receive a definition: what did it mean? AXA argued that it bore its ordinary meaning – that AXA had incurred a liability whether or not it had made a payment in respect of that liability. Genworth contended that it must mean that AXA had actually made a payment in respect of that liability, not just that it had become liable to do so.

As we have seen above, Bryan J decided that this was not an indemnity, rather an obligation in the nature of an on demand payment obligation, though the decision is still of interest for indemnity provisions. He held that "incurred" did not import that AXA had to prove actual payment and that it would suffice if the liability existed without AXA having (necessarily) paid out yet to the successful claimant. Indeed, in some instances, AXA had issued cheques in respect of a liability and those cheques had never been encashed and might never be. Bryan J rejected the idea that AXA would thereby be receiving a windfall: there was "good commercial sense" in AXA being able to be put in funds "on demand" before it had itself paid out on the relevant liability.

Of course, *AXA v Genworth* is not strictly speaking a case on indemnities but does illustrate a possible ambiguity in wording typically found in indemnity drafting. From these two cases (Minera and AXA), use of "payable" and "incurred" respectively led to an ambiguity. Why should this be so?

The classic example of the approach taken by the courts with regard to liability under indemnities can be found in *Firma C-Trade SA v Newcastle P&I Association (The 'Fanti' and 'The Padre Island')* [1991]

2 AC 1. This involved what were effectively insurance contracts (i.e. contracts of indemnity) taken out by a shipowner with a P&I Club but the House of Lords also considered the situation in contracts of indemnity in general. It is one of the foundational cases when construing indemnities. There were two conjoined appeals to the House of Lords relating to two different vessels, with both cases involving very similar facts. Take the case of the Fanti. She had departed on a voyage containing a cargo of cement owned by Firma C-Trade, but she developed a leak and was towed to Cascais in Portugal where she was abandoned to salvors. Firma C-Trade as cargo owner obtained default judgment against the Fanti's owner, but the owner never paid the judgment debt and was ordered to be wound up. The relevant policy in favour of the Fanti's owner provided,

> "The [vessel's owner] shall be protected and indemnified against all or any of the following claims and expenses which he shall have become liable to pay and shall in fact have paid ... (q) For loss or damage caused to ... property ... carried on board a ship entered in this class ... "

What the cargo owners alleged in these appeals was as follows. Pursuant to the Third Parties (Rights against Insurers) Act 1930, any rights of the insolvent insured against the insurer at the time of insolvency were transferred to the person claiming against the insolvent insured. The question then turned to what rights the ship owners in these cases actually had against their P&I Clubs – in other words, what rights were there that could be transferred to the cargo owners?

At this point, some legal history must, regrettably, be related. Prior to the Judicature Acts of 1873-5, law and equity were separate and they each treated indemnities differently. The common law could only order damages, so there had to be an actual liability before the common law could (arguably) be engaged, with some cases going so far as to suggest that the indemnifier would only be liable for damages in a court of common law if the indemnified had first satisfied the liability to the third party. However, at equity, a contract of indemnity could be enforced by specific performance or a declaration, the former remedy ordering the indemnifier to pay the amount due under the indemnity either to the creditor or, perhaps, to the indemnified. The Judicature Acts provided for the fusion of law and equity and further provided that equity should prevail.

With that by way of background, the argument developed by the cargo owners was to the effect that the insolvent insureds could be seen in equity as having contingent rights against their respective P&I Clubs, and these contingent rights were capable of being transferred to the claimants under the 1930 Act. This would enable the cargo owners to proceed against the P&I Clubs using the contingent rights transferred from the insolvent insureds.

Given this ingenious argument, the House of Lords had to consider the situation more generally, looking beyond the area of insurance, looking therefore more generally at indemnities and how they were treated at common law and in equity. The terms of the contract with the P&I Club made it clear that payment out by the insured ("*shall have become liable to pay and shall in fact have paid*") was a precondition for receiving a vested right to indemnity. The House of Lords upheld the common law's approach to an indemnity, namely, that the indemnified got no cause of action until he had suffered an actual loss. The indemnifier can only be in breach of contract after a loss is suffered or an expense incurred by the indemnified. As against which, looking at it through the eyes of equity, there was nothing that could be specifically enforced – the express provisions of the P&I Club's terms made it clear that no liability arose until the liability had both arisen and been paid by the insured. Even though the Judicature Acts made it clear that equity would prevail over the rules of common law, in this case, equity could not intervene as the time for its involvement had not yet come. If there had been an actual obligation to pay, that would be different: in this case, there was no obligation to pay.

This takes many lawyers by surprise. There is a general feeling that an indemnity is an obligation on the part of the indemnifier to take on the primary responsibility for taking practical steps to deal with (in the sense of disputing or paying off) any loss or expense within the scope of the indemnity, but this is not the general approach of the courts in ruling on indemnities. Of course, it would be possible to make express provision for such a different result, but this would require specific wording. Reference to the *Minera* case above showed that, faced with ambiguity in the wording, the courts will fall back on what is now a fairly well established approach in indemnity cases.

An example of where *Firma C-Trade* was applied can be seen in *Aluflet v Vinave Empresa de Navegaçao Maritima (The Faial)* [2000] 1 Lloyds Rep 473. The somewhat complex facts can be summarised as follows. Aluflet, the shipowner, chartered the "Xove" to the defendant charterers for three years under a bareboat charter (i.e. a contract whereby the charterer would take over complete control of the operation of the vessel for the duration of the contract). The relevant indemnity provided,

> "*In the event of the Vessel becoming a wreck or obstruction to navigation the Charterers shall indemnify the Owners against*

any sums whatsoever which the Owners shall become liable to
pay and shall pay in consequence of the Vessel becoming a wreck
or obstruction in navigation."

Less than a week after the commencement of the charterparty, the Xove capsized and sank, becoming, without any doubt, a *"wreck or obstruction to navigation"* and the parties were agreed that the contract had come to an end at that point. The harbour authorities required the wreck to be removed and it was removed by the shipowner at no little expense, these expenses starting some two months after the sinking and continuing for a period of just over six months. The shipowners, relying on a specific provision in the contract, purported to arrest a different vessel owned by the charterers and relied on the charterer's breach of the indemnity to support that arrest.

The question for the court was whether the indemnity applied to the facts that had happened: only if the claimant shipowner had a vested right to indemnity could the court uphold the arrest of the separate vessel belonging to the charterer. The judge found from the clause no fewer than three conditions precedent: first, that there was a wreck or obstruction to navigation; secondly, that the owners were liable to pay sums for removal of the wreck and thirdly, that the owners had actually paid those sums.

Everyone agreed that the first of these conditions had been met: the ship had sunk and was in everyone's way. However, the third condition was not met: at the time of the shipowner's claim to arrest the charterer's other vessel, its claim to indemnity had not vested as it had not in fact paid any sums for the removal of the wreck. The judge, however, was equivocal on the second condition: the judge had no evidence as to when the liability had *"first become ascertained and established even if not ultimately quantified"*. This was an open question – to what extent must a claim to indemnity be established: that it was a theoretical claim, a sound claim, or a sound claim to a specific and quantified amount of money? This point was left open – the judge's decision on the third point was sufficient to dispose of the case and in this he was following the decision of the House of Lords in *Firma C-Trade.*

The establishment of the time when an indemnity becomes effective is important not only for the parties when carrying out the terms of an indemnity (when do I get paid? when do I have to pay?) but can also be critical for e.g. limitation purposes. To what extent must an indemnified be able to point to a precisely quantified liability before being able to claim that amount under an indemnity covering that loss? Everything will come down to the precise language of the indemnity and ordinary rules of construction will apply.

An interesting example is the Scottish case of *Scott Lithgow v Secretary of State for Defence* 1989 SC (HL) 9. The MOD contracted with Scott Lithgow for the construction of two submarines. The contract required the use of certain pressure tight cables which were in turn to be supplied by certain manufacturers. Scott Lithgow sourced the cables from BICC, which was an approved manufacturer for this purpose, but the cables proved to be inadequate after installation started. Scott Lithgow claimed as against BICC and then sought indemnity from the MOD under clause 15 of the contract. This provided in clause 15(1) for the MOD to indemnify Scott Lithgow against loss, damage and liability suffered or incurred by it but then provided in clause 15(5) as follows,

> *"In the event of incident whereby loss, damage or liability may result in a claim under the indemnity, [Scott Lithgow] should report the circumstances of the incident to the principal naval*

overseer immediately and, in the interests of prompt settlement, should submit [its] priced claim as soon as possible thereafter. An estimate of the cost of replacement, repair or liability is to be included in the initial notification of the incident or submitted within 14 days thereafter."

The claim under the indemnity was made some five years after the cables were found to be defective, five years being the limitation period applicable in Scotland. The question of Scottish Law for the House of Lords was when the claim under the indemnity became enforceable which would determine when the limitation period started to run. There were various candidates for this point of time: it might be when the cables were first found to be defective or it might be when Scott Lithgow had complied with the rather vacuous terms of clause 15(5).

Scott Lithgow of course argued that the indemnity became enforceable when it had submitted a priced claim according to clause 15(5). The parties were agreed that Scott Lithgow had submitted a priced claim compliant with clause 15(5) and had done so within the five year limitation period. Naturally, the MOD contended that the indemnity became enforceable when the cables were discovered to be defective, which was outside the five year limitation period.

So what was the effect of clause 15(5): was compliance with it some sort of condition precedent to recovery under the indemnity? The arbitrator and the court on appeal found that clause 15(5) did exist as a sort of condition precedent, so bringing Scott Lithgow's claim within the limitation period.

The House of Lords disagreed. The use in clause 15(5) of "should report" and "should submit" were not words of obligation, and the inclusion of "as soon as possible" militated against clause 15(5) being a condition precedent as the wording was simply too vague. Rather, clause 15(5) should be seen as having an administrative character, simply providing useful information to Scott Lithgow on how to make its claim. It was not a concern to the House of Lords that the claim might have to be made while still not capable of precise quantification and this is the important point to be derived from this decision. As with all cases on indemnities, it is not an inflexible rule of law, but an interesting illustration of how one particular indemnity was applied (and how others might be applied).

A more recent discussion in the English courts can be seen in *Cape Distribution v Cape Intermediate Holdings* [2016] EWHC 1786 (QB). This was major litigation concerning liability for employees' and former employees' asbestos related illnesses. In 1964, there was a sale agreement whereby Cape Distribution (CDL) transferred its business to Cape Intermediate Holdings (CIH) against an indemnity given by CIH in CDL's favour. CDL had been operating an asbestos manufacturing facility. Following the sale agreement, CDL continued to operate, but this time as agent for CIH.

There were two indemnities of possible relevance in the sale agreement. The first read as follows,

> "*As part of the consideration for the said sale [CIH] shall undertake pay satisfy and discharge all the debts liabilities and obligations (including all income tax and profits tax assessable by reference to profits up to the Time of Sale) of [CDL] whatsoever subsisting at the Time of Sale and shall adopt perform and fulfil all contracts and engagements binding on [CDL] at the Time of Sale and shall at all times keep [CDL] indemnified against the*

same and against all proceedings costs and demands in respect thereof."

The second read,

"Until the completion of the sale [CDL] shall carry on the business of [CDL] as heretofore and shall in so doing be deemed to be the agent of [CIH] and shall account and be entitled to be indemnified accordingly."

Again, there are various candidates for the honour of being the start date for the enforceability of of these indemnities:

- The date when each employee established liability (whether by judgment, award or settlement) – CDL contended for this date as it gave it the longest possible period of time in which to claim under the indemnity

- The date when any employee made a claim for compensation against CDL – CIH contended for this date as it had the potential for making more indemnity claims time-barred

- The date when CDL's liability to any particular employee accrued

- The date when an employee received a payment from CDL

Neither party contended for either of the latter two options, though they have been considered and upheld in different cases, as will shortly be seen.

For Picken J, after reviewing the authorities in this area, the matter ultimately came down to a question of construction of the indemnity in question, and there are no general rules of law applicable to indemnities of one type or another. Different authorities have come to different conclusions based on the specific wording of the indemnity in question, so –

- The date of accrual was found to be the correct time in *Bosma v Larsen* [1966] 1 Lloyd's Rep. 22 – this was an indemnity in respect of *"all consequences or liabilities arising"*

- The date of payment was the correct time in the *Firma C-Trade* – mandated by the wording *"... and shall in fact have paid"*

By and large, the authorities have not been kind to the approach of McNair J in *Bosma v Larsen*, and the date of accrual appears to have been a somewhat rare finding for the enforceability of an indemnity.

After a detailed examination of the wording and taking account of the surrounding circumstances, Picken J held that CDL's contention was correct – that the indemnity became enforceable for limitation purposes when each employee managed to establish liability, regardless of payment by CDL. Picken J highlighted a number of factors to support this finding, principally that the use of the words *"shall undertake pay satisfy and discharge"* tended to show that there had to be an established or realised liability, not a mere assertion of a claim.

As we have seen, therefore, there are no fixed rules applicable to indemnities which in turn means that there are some potential problems both for the indemnifier and the indemnified, especially in the context of an indemnity against liabilities to third parties, and various question arise for consideration:

- Must the indemnified first pay the third party before making a claim under the indemnity?

- Is it sufficient that the liability of the indemnified to the third party has arisen or that it has been proved? To what standard?

- Whom should the indemnifier pay – the indemnified or the third party?

- What is the correct remedy to claim: debt, damages or specific performance?

- If payment is to be made to the indemnified, is the indemnifier concerned to ensure that the money is then paid over to the third party or can the indemnified apply the funds elsewhere at its discretion?

These are all interesting questions but the law does not provide precise answers because everything will depend on the wording. From the drafting point of view, the answer is obvious: all these questions need to be considered at the drafting stage. One problem is that draftsmen insist on piling up tired expressions such as "hold harmless" in apparent ignorance of the fact that these expressions do not have a core meaning and will not determine the essential questions posed above.

These points were considered recently in the complex case of *Durley House v Firmdale Hotels* [2014] EWHC 2608 (Ch). The facts are striking and caused the judge to address head on the questions posed above and to consider how best to apply the *Firma C-Trade* case.

Durley House was the lessee of premises in Sloane Street, London which it sublet to Firmdale Hotels. Firmdale Hotels was obliged to pay rent under the lease to the lessor, Cadogan Estates and indemnified Durley House against any failure to pay rent.

With rent unpaid by Durley House, the lessor (Cadogan Estates) brought possession proceedings against Durley House and forfeited the lease, getting an order for the payment of outstanding rent and damages. Durley House's only asset had been the lease and it had no other assets with which it could pay the sums adjudged due. The judgment therefore remained unpaid and Durley House went into insolvency. Subsequently, Durley House and Cadogan Estates entered into a settlement agreement to the effect that Durley House would pay over to Cadogan Estates the "net recovery" it made in proceedings against Firmdale Hotels in return for the discharge of all other liabilities it had to Cadogan Estates.

Various questions arose including whether Firmdale had any outstanding liabilities to Durley House under the indemnity given that Durley House had made no payment to Cadogan Estates and given also that the settlement agreement seemed to indicate that it had no outstanding liability to pay anyway. Firmdale Hotels argued that payment by Durley House to Cadogan Estates was a precondition to recovery under the indemnity.

The judge construed the settlement agreement as between Cadogan Estates and Durley House as having the effect that there was still an existing liability on the part of Durley House to pay the sums adjudged due and that the settlement agreement only took effect as a stay on enforcement, not a discharge. However, the question remained whether Durley House could recover under the indemnity, notwithstanding that it had not yet paid Cadogan Estates.

After a comprehensive review of sometimes conflicting authorities going back to *Collinge v Haywood* in the 1830's, the judge drew a number of conclusions. If these are correct and are followed in future, they represent a great step forward in our understanding of contractual indemnities and contain useful pointers for drafting and enforcement. In summary, the judge's conclusions are as follows:

- Prior to the Judicature Acts of 1873-5, the courts of common law and equity applied different rules to indemnities, with the consequence that the common law (arguably) required actual payment out before an action could be maintained on an indemnity: since then equity has prevailed and there is no requirement that payment should be made before the indemnified can recover under an indemnity

- Even at common law, the position is not clear: one view is that an obligation to "hold harmless" the indemnified meant that the indemnifier had to prevent the loss or arising arising in the first place rather than to reimburse the indemnified after the latter had paid out; however, the action for breach of an indemnity is an action for damages, not in debt

- Be that all as it may, in equity the indemnified could always claim a remedy under an indemnity even before payment had been made to the third party creditor and this remains true even if the indemnifier did not undertake to pay the third party creditor directly: in these cases the court can order the indemnifier to make a payment to the third party creditor directly or pay the money into a separate fund

- There is some support in the cases for the idea that the court can order the indemnifier to make a payment direct to the indemnified, not to the creditor, at least "in some cases"[17]

---

[17] See Lord Brandon's speech in *Firma C-Trade*

although the proper principle derived from the cases could well be that there is no limitation on this

- There is no difference between cases on contractual indemnities and cases on contracts of indemnity insurance

The upshot of the application of these principles was that the indemnifier was liable in damages for its failure to indemnify, and an order could be made for the indemnifier (Firmdale Hotels) to pay the indemnified (Durley House) directly: it was not a concern of Firmdale Hotels as indemnifier to see that the money it paid was then paid to the creditor (Cadogan Estates).

The points above have been presented as they are given in the judgment but, in order to do so, the deputy judge[18] had to tread carefully through a number of old and, to some extent, inconsistent decisions. This must be borne in mind before simply taking the above principles as settled law. There is no "law of indemnities" as such, simply decisions responding to the words and circumstances of each individual case. From the commercial lawyer's point of view, it is submitted that the best course would be to make the above points clear in the drafting rather than leaving them to the vagaries of judicial scrutiny as the matter is not necessarily beyond doubt.

Having said which, the judge's piecing together of the various judgments to come up with the principles described above is ingenious, and moreover ends up with a statement of principles that is both commercially sensible and coherent. It is to be hoped that, in future cases, this case will be the foundation for further decisions applying these

---

[18] Stephen Morris QC sitting as a Deputy High Court judge.

principles – but this is a statement of hope, not a statement of existing, settled law.

Practice point

Surprisingly many indemnities are drafted with scant regard for what is perhaps the most important point for both indemnifier and indemnified: just when must the money be handed over? Deriving from this is a subsidiary question: just how detailed must a claim be? Should it be capable of precise quantification, or can an estimated claim suffice? This might be important for limitation purposes. The indemnified might be concerned to be put in funds before paying out on an indemnified third party claim, but this needs to be stated expressly.

The drafting points are simple:

- Make it clear when the indemnity is intended to "bite" – exactly when must the indemnifier pay the indemnified and when exactly must the parties take any steps specified in the conduct of indemnity provision?
- If any steps are intended to be a condition precedent, then this should be stated expressly

How is the money received under the indemnity applied?

Following the lengthy discussion of *Durley House* above, one question to which the judge seemed to assume the answer was whether the indemnified, on receiving funds paid under an indemnity, was bound to apply that money to payment of the creditor. The court in that case thought that the indemnified recipient of the money from the indemnifier could dispose of it as it wished: the indemnifier had no interest in how the money should be applied. The answer may not be that easy as there could be reasons why the creditor and the indemnifier are interested in seeing that it is applied by payment directly to the creditor.

Take the situation where the indemnified has two separate creditors each for £1,000. There is an indemnity in respect of the debt owed to one creditor, but not to the other. The indemnified claims under the indemnity for payment of one creditor but all along intends to use the money to pay off the other creditor. Is the indemnifier bound to pay, regardless of the fact that the money paid under the indemnity will not be used to satisfy the debt being indemnified?

There could be many reasons why the various parties are each interested in the outcome: if the indemnified is insolvent, the creditors may never see the money. Absent insolvency, the indemnified may have no intention of paying either creditor and the money paid under the indemnity may be dissipated by the indemnified on other things. Equity could get around this by ordering specific performance of the indemnity in favour of the particular creditor, thus ensuring that the money bypasses the indemnified completely. If, however, the indemnified sues the indemnifier for damages, what then?

In the area of contractual indemnities, there is no clear answer from the cases, as there is no clear answer in the area of general damages. This latter point is illustrated in the classic case on the point, *Ruxley Electronics & Construction v Forsyth* [1996] AC 344. Ruxley was contracted to build a swimming pool for Forsyth to a specification requiring a depth at the diving end of seven feet six inches. In fact, it was finished only to a depth of six feet: there was no evidence that the pool as built was unsuitable for diving. Forsyth wanted to rebuild the pool in its entirety to get a pool to the specifications he had set. However, the House of Lords disagreed, saying that the cost would be out of all proportion to the benefit he would obtain. The trial judge had not been convinced that Forsyth would in fact allocate the damages to the work of rebuilding but, on appeal, Forsyth gave an undertaking to the effect that he would in fact do so. Lords Lloyd and Jauncey expressed the view that the court is not normally concerned with what a claimant does with the damages awarded, although whether or not the claimant intends to adopt the more costly of two options may be relevant in assessing its reasonableness.

This case (and others) was considered in the context of a contract of indemnity insurance which, as we have seen from *Durley House* which we considered above, is in many ways to be equated to a contractual (non-insurance) contract of indemnity. In *Endurance Corporate Capital v Sartex Quilts and Textiles* [2020] EWCA Civ 308, Sartex was the insured owner of industrial premises which it intended for the manufacture of certain textile products. Endurance was the underwriter of the relevant policy. There was a fire in 2011 which caused serious damage to the premises. Prior to that, Sartex had been acquiring all the machinery and equipment it would need to open the factory. By the time of the fire, one production line was up and running, while the other two were awaiting the installation of an upgraded electricity supply before they could begin.

Sartex made claims for both property loss and business interruption, liability for the latter of which Endurance accepted liability. Endurance paid out on the business interruption claim but the parties could not agree on the correct basis for calculating the property loss. Sartex said that the correct basis was the reinstatement value of the property while Endurance said that the correct basis was the lower diminution in market value of the property, which was the sum Endurance paid to Sartex.

The trial judge found as a fact that Sartex intended to use the premises for the purpose of manufacturing textiles. However, by the time of the trial itself some eight years later, no rebuilding work had even started, and work had not commenced on textile production at the insured premises or elsewhere. The trial judge's findings were complicated: immediately after the fire, Sartex did intend to reinstate the premises but then looked at other options for the manufacture of the textiles. As regards the premises themselves, at one point Sartex considered reinstating them for the purpose of opening a banqueting centre (for which local authority permission was refused). By 2018, the trial judge found that Sartex had the intention of reinstating the premises and re-commencing manufacture. The judge found for Sartex and awarded the reinstatement value both of the premises and the machinery.

The policy's wording was convoluted and in effect provided that Sartex could not recover more than the general law would allow. The question therefore was, what does the general law allow as the correct measure?

On this the principles of the law are not in great dispute and were set out by Leggatt LJ. The indemnity insurance takes effect as a promise that the insured will not suffer the loss indemnified against, so that when the loss occurs, it is treated as a breach of contract and the insured is entitled to be put in the position he would have been in if the loss had not occurred. Of course, where the loss is property, the loss can be calculated as being either the cost of repair or replacement or it could be the diminished value of the property minus any residual value. Which measure is used depends on the circumstances: if the insured intended to use the premises, the measure will normally be the cost of repair or replacement whereas if he intended to sell the premises, the measure will normally be the reduction in market value of the premises.

The judge had awarded compensation on the basis that Sartex would reconstruct the premises in the same general shape and style as the old but using cheaper modern materials. The Court of Appeal agreed: there was no evidence that Sartex would sell the premises and no evidence of any alternative premises that would be cheaper to build and kit out. Equally, there was no evidence that the value of the premises had actually increased (e.g. as a result of losing listed status, as is the situation in some cases). That all being so, the question of Sartex' intentions was irrelevant and it was simply a question of valuing the loss, which was the reinstatement value, not the diminution in value of the premises.

The insured's intention with regard to the money to be paid by the insurer may be relevant, but it seems only in a few situations as shown by the cases as discussed in the *Sartex* case e.g.

- There may be specific characteristics concerning the property such as its being historic and more expensive to reinstate to the original conditions (see *Reynolds v Phoenix Assurance Co Ltd* [1978] 2 Lloyd's Rep 440)

- The property may actually increase in value as a result of the event triggering the indemnity such as by losing listed building status and becoming more suitable for redevelopment (see *Great Lakes Reinsurance (UK) SE v Western Trading Ltd* [2016] EWCA Civ 1003)

Of course, insurance policies often get around this problem because they state expressly the basis of the calculation of the indemnity: for example, an insured with a home contents policy will these days normally be looking for "new for old" compensation. By extension, the same principles are applicable to contractual (non-insurance) indemnities but, unlike insurance cases, rarely is it stated how the value of the indemnity is to be calculated: is it effectively a blank cheque for the indemnified, or is there some principle of reasonableness based on the indemnified's intentions with regard to the sum to be paid under the indemnity? Sometimes, a contractual indemnity does state the basis of compensation but this can create its own problems: in Chapter Six, we look at the case of *MAN Nutzfahrzeuge v Freightliner* [2005] EWHC 2347 (Comm) and we will see how a simple definition of "Damages" in the context of an indemnity led to such complex litigation.

It will be necessary to come back to this question in the next chapter. For the moment, it is enough to note the following possibilities with regard to contractual indemnities:

- It is likely the case that the indemnified need not have actually incurred the expense which is the subject of the indemnity, but there has to be an actual, not a contingent, liability (see *Durley House v Firmdale Hotels* [2014] EWHC 2608 (Ch))

- If the indemnified has actually incurred the expense and is now claiming it under the indemnity then, in principle, there is nothing to prevent recovery under the indemnity provided that it is within the scope of the indemnity as drafted

- The more interesting question is whether mitigation should apply to the question of recovery, which is a question to be addressed in the following chapter; in the normal non-indemnity case, where a claimant takes steps to remedy or mitigate the consequences of a breach of contract, then it is entitled to recover the costs of those steps unless there is a cheaper option which it was reasonable to expect the claimant to take (see paragraph 61 of *Endurance Corporate Capital v Sartex Quilts and Textiles* [2020] EWCA Civ 308)

- If the claimant has taken no steps to remedy or mitigate by the time the court comes to assess the value of the indemnity, the claimant's intention is only relevant if there is a dispute about what it is reasonable to expect the claimant to do to put himself in a materially equivalent position as if the breach of contract (i.e. the event triggering the indemnity) had never occurred (see paragraph 62 of *Endurance Corporate Capital v Sartex Quilts and Textiles* [2020] EWCA Civ 308)

- Deriving from the insurance cases including *Endurance Corporate Capital v Sartex Quilts and Textiles* [2020] EWCA Civ 308 and the cases referred to therein, there may be situations where there are different and rival bases for assessing the value of the indemnity depending on the particular circumstances – so it could be reinstatement or diminution in value in the property cases, and there could be other bases in contractual indemnities covering other situations

Given the relative paucity of cases in the field of contractual (non-insurance) indemnities it is not possible to state these rules with more precision. It is part and parcel of the treatment of the scope of the indemnity. To what extent can the indemnified sit back and allow losses to mount and then claim complete reimbursement from the indemnifier? When we see how the cases in fact address the level of recovery under an indemnity by considering the scope of a contractual indemnity, then it is possible to observe that the scope of the indemnity is sometimes used as a means of limiting recovery under it.

Settlement of an indemnified liability

Where the indemnified is indemnified against a liability to a third party, it may of course decide to come to terms with that third party by agreeing to pay compensation in settlement of the third party's claim. The question then arises whether the indemnified may claim from the indemnifier the sum agreed with the third party.

The short answer is that it may and this principle is illustrated in a number of cases. Of course, the position may be different in the specific indemnity's wording, which may allow the indemnifier the right to take over sole conduct of the defence and to be responsible for settlement of any sums. Whether this counts as a condition precedent to recovery under the indemnity will be a question of construction, as was seen with the "ticket to ride" cases discussed in Chapter Two. The following cases illustrate the general position where there is no express wording in the indemnity dealing with this situation.

In *Comyn Ching v Oriental Tube* (1979) 17 BLR 47 (CA), Comyn Ching was a subcontractor on a contract for the erection of two halls of residence for Queen Mary College. The architect retained by the College mandated the use of a certain type of plastic coated steel piping manufactured by Oriental Tube. Comyn Ching was uncertain about the qualities of this piping and entered into correspondence with Oriental Tube. In the course of that correspondence, Oriental Tube confirmed to Comyn Ching in a letter which was held to have contractual effect,

> " ... *we are prepared to accept responsibility for your own company's future liabilities in every sense of the word.*"

It may be noted that the word "indemnity" is not used: it is another example of what was referred to above as a "quasi-indemnity": wording which has more or less the same effect as an indemnity, but without actually using that word.

With its doubts assuaged, Comyn Ching continued to incorporate the piping manufactured by Oriental Tube. The piping was inadequate and almost immediately cracked causing leaks. Comyn Ching attempted repairs but this proved ineffective and so Comyn Ching went ahead and replaced the whole system.

Comyn Ching found itself in litigation with the College and, in a compromise of that dispute, agreed to pay the College one third of the damages claimed plus costs and Comyn Ching further agreed to abandon its counterclaim against the main contractor and paid part of its costs too.

The Court of Appeal reflected on the perils of litigation, noting that the College's claim for breach of warranty was not certain, while its claim for negligence could well have succeeded. In any case, it would have been costly for Comyn Ching to defend. It found that it was reasonable to settle the litigation and the amount involved in the compromise was a reasonable one (relying on *Biggin v Permanite* [1951] 2 KB 314). The result was that Comyn Ching could recover the damages and costs agreed to be paid to Oriental Tube under the "quasi-indemnity" wording given as set out in the letter.

A more perhaps borderline case can be seen in *General Feeds v Slobodna Plovidba Yugoslavia* [1999] 1 Lloyds Rep 688. General Feeds chartered the Krapan J from Slobodna to carry a cargo from Peru to China. The cargo arrived damaged by heat, fire and smoke but there was a dispute as to how this had come about: the insurers claimed that the cause was bad stowage whereas Slobodna asserted that it arose from the state of the cargo when loaded. The basis of Slobodna's claim was under Article IV Rule 6 of the Hague-Visby Rules providing an indemnity in the case of loading of dangerous cargo,

> "... the shipper of [inflammable, explosive or dangerous] goods shall be liable for all damages and expenses directly or indirectly arising out of or resulting from such shipment. ..."

Again, this is what this book calls a "quasi-indemnity": the word "indemnity" itself has not been used but the effect for practical purposes is the same.

However, General Feeds pointed to the weight of the evidence suggesting that the reason for the state of the cargo was its condition on loading. Accordingly, it argued that the settlement was unreasonable. Upon appeal from an arbitral award, the court again pointed to *Biggin v Permanite* [1951] 2 KB 314 to the effect that both the fact and the amount of the settlement must be reasonable. The court noted that a claim could be weak but might be settled to avoid an expensive trial: unless it appeared that a claim was so weak that no reasonable shipowner or P&I Club would take it seriously, it could not be said that the loss attributable to a reasonable settlement was not caused by the breach. Overall, it was necessary to have regard to the facts understood at the time of the settlement. It was held that the arbitrators had applied the right law and so their decision to uphold the settlement figure was upheld.

On reading the judgement, one possible feeling is that the claimant was lucky to win on its claim under the "quasi-indemnity" for such a settlement. Alternatively, it could be argued that this case demonstrates the willingness of a court to show some leniency to a claimant which finds itself stuck in a dispute and facing a mass of evidence, some of which at least is harmful to its case. The courts adopt an approach that could be said to be sympathetic to the settlement of disputes and perhaps this case is one more example of this. It is also a case of an appeal from an award, where the court was less concerned with rehearing the evidence but rather with verifying that the tribunal had applied the right principles of law.

Megarry J once said that the law reports were charts of the wrecks of unsinkable cases; in other words, parties could start a trial buoyed up with hopes of a successful outcome based on watertight evidence and legal advice, only to find their hopes dashed against the rocks by the vagaries of the trial process. This directly informs the attitude taken by the courts to settlements of disputes, effectively taking a "hands off" approach unless it is clear that the party agreeing to the settlement was behaving manifestly unreasonably.

A more recent example of the latitude given by the courts to the claimant is shown by *Supershield v Siemens Building Technologies* [2010] EWCA Civ 7. Here, a nut and bolt connection, for which Supershield was contractually responsible to Siemens, failed. Siemens settled the claim for the damage caused by the resulting flood for some £2.8 million, which it claimed against Supershield. The Court of Appeal noted that a "settlement value" is not an objective fact – there is no available market for such things. In reality, it is a subjective opinion taking account of many variables. The role of the trial judge is not to find whether a particular settlement figure was objectively reasonable in the sense that he would have assessed liability at that sum, but whether the settlement figure fell within the range of what might be considered "reasonable". The court noted the intricate arguments around causation and remoteness – that the flood would not have occurred if the drains had not been blocked by packaging, that the escape of water was too remote a consequence, added to which there was an absence of monitoring of the equipment. The argument was that the strength of these points was not reflected in the actual settlement.

The Court of Appeal noted that *"it would have been a rash lawyer who would have advised Siemens that it was likely to succeed on the causation issue, let alone that it could be confident of doing so"*. After considering the law of remoteness, the Court of Appeal simply concluded that,

> *"Siemens had only to show that it was reasonable to settle the claims made against it as it did. I see no proper reason for overturning the judge's conclusion that it was reasonable."*

While not actually a case on an indemnity, the same principle will (or in theory should) apply, and so the decision in *General Feeds* becomes more comprehensible. Where an indemnity is provided against a liability to a third party, absent any express provisions dealing with the indemnifier having the right to have sole conduct of the defence or any right to veto a proposed settlement, the indemnified has quite a degree of latitude in dealing with and settling the third party claim. It does not have to show that it has arrived at a settlement that was objectively reasonable, rather that it was reasonable to settle and that the agreed figure was reasonable – "reasonable" being used here not in the sense of "objectively reasonable" but rather "reasonable for this party in this situation facing possibly complex, expensive and uncertain litigation with, to a greater or lesser extent, an unpredictable result".

Practice points

This discussion in fact leads neatly to the next section: what exactly then is a "liability"? This section should be read in conjunction with the following section therefore.

For present purposes, an indemnified may have all sorts of reasons to dispose of a claim against it, some relating to the strength of the claim, others relating to the indemnified's own position (such as its desire to avoid negative publicity). It would appear from the above that a decision to settle is a discretion vested in the indemnified, not an obligation to come to a result that is in all the circumstances an objectively reasonable one. The distinction between the two was neatly illustrated recently in *Lehman Brothers Special Financing v National Power Corp* [2018] EWHC 487 (Comm). As noted in that case, a discretion to be exercised reasonably and an obligation to come to an objectively reasonable result are different while both may result in a range of two extremes from which a particular figure could be chosen. While none of the authorities puts it this way, the courts give more "latitude" to a party vested with a discretion: this can be seen perhaps in both *General Feeds v Slobodna Plovidba Yugoslavia* [1999] 1 Lloyds Rep 688 and *Supershield v Siemens Building Technologies* [2010] EWCA Civ 7, discussed immediately above.

If the indemnified is vested with authority to settle a claim and then claim the sum settled (perhaps with other costs and expenses) under the indemnity, the following appear to be the at least the points to cover in drafting:

- Is the indemnified entitled to exercise its discretion in coming to a reasonable settlement or is it obliged to come to an objectively reasonable settlement?

- If a discretion, what are the factors to be taken into account in assessing reasonableness, in particular, to what extent can it take its own circumstances into account?

- If an obligation to come to an objectively reasonable settlement, who would assess that reasonableness and what factors are to be taken into account – obviously the strength or weakness of the third party's claim, but is anything else (such as the indemnified's own circumstances) to be taken into account?

- What is the involvement of the indemnifier in this whole process: is notice of a third party claim to be given and is it a condition precedent to recovery under the indemnity? What is the point of giving notice: what powers of authorisation or veto are to be vested in the indemnifier and, again, what factors are to be taken into account when the indemnifier exercises this discretion?

What is a "liability"?

It is now necessary to take a look at the astonishing facts of *Rust Consulting v PB Limited* [2012] EWCA Civ 1070 and how that case fared on its travels through the High Court (twice) and into final resolution in the Court of Appeal (twice). This again should act as a correction to those lawyers who think that having the protection of an indemnity will of itself make recovery easier or quicker. The facts of this case were called "astonishing" above as the case stands as a stark warning to lawyers inserting indemnities without thought for the consequences of doing so.

Parson Brinckerhoff was a worldwide group headquartered in the USA. The group ultimately owned both PB Limited and Rust Consulting. Rust had been an engineering company engaged in 1995 by a third party, Eagle, to do some work on a shopping centre, which it did.

In 1996, Rust ceased to trade and later in 1997, Rust and PB entered into an intra-group asset purchase agreement whereby Rust sold its assets to PB and PB assumed all of Rust's outstanding liabilities and obligations. The wording was in this form,

> "The consideration for the sale and transfer by [Rust] [...] is (i) the sum of £1,000 and (ii) [PB] assuming responsibility for the satisfaction, fulfilment and discharge of all of the Liabilities and the Contracts of the Business outstanding at the Effective Date and [PB] hereby indemnifies and covenants to keep indemnified [Rust] against all proceedings, claims and demands in respect thereof."

Matters might have rested there but, ten years later, in 2007, Eagle notified a claim in negligence against Rust for its work on the shopping centre, claiming some £8 million in damages plus interest. Of course, Rust had no assets with which to defend, let alone satisfy, the claim. It incurred some legal costs, paid for by the Parsons Brinckerhoff group, and then went into a creditors' liquidation, the creditors of course being the Parsons Brinckerhoff group. The liquidators told Eagle that they thought its claim was inflated but that Rust had no assets or insurance, and so they consented to judgment in the sum claimed by Eagle of £8m. As it ultimately became clear from the evidence, the Parsons Brinckerhoff group was more concerned with its insurance position: with a deductible of US$15 million against a fluctuating exchange rate, it perceived a risk that its group insurers might become involved and defend the case leading to further costs and expenses. The group therefore took the decision not to defend the case on the basis that (it believed on advice) it would have no liability to satisfy Eagle's judgment anyway.

Matters might have rested there too, but Eagle, now the majority creditor with a judgment in its favour, replaced the existing liquidators with others more sympathetic to its cause. At this point, the indemnity in the asset purchase agreement came to light: Rust, in other words, did have an asset and a very valuable one at that – it had the benefit of the indemnity given by PB!

One question to be answered was this: what was a "liability"? If a party simply consents to judgment without any detailed consideration of the claim or the evidence, can that sum simply be passed down the chain so to speak and claimed under an indemnity? Remember, this was not in any way a compromise of the litigation, it was waving the white flag and giving the third party claimant everything it was asking for without any detailed consideration of the claim, any detailed assessment of the evidence or taking any serious account at all of the perils of litigation as they might affect either the claimant or the defendant.

Did the consent judgment amount to a "liability" or was it necessary for Rust's liquidators, not only to prove the fact of the consent judgment, but also to go on to prove that there was in any case an underlying liability to support the consent judgment?

The first instance judgment given by Akenhead J ([2010] EWHC 3243 (TCC)) is of great interest as it goes through a number of old cases on indemnities going back to 1789: as stated at the beginning of this book indemnities are not new inventions of commercial drafting. As a straight matter of construction, Akenhead J held that the indemnity covered

Rust's potential liability to Eagle. However, the next question was whether the consent judgment obtained by Eagle against Rust meant that Rust's liquidators could, without more, claim the amount of the judgment under the indemnity. Akenhead J went further, saying,

> *"The fact that proceedings were issued against Rust by [Eagle] in relation to the relevant [construction works] does not of itself mean that PB was liable to indemnify Rust against them; similarly, simply because a judgement had been entered against Rust, and even if after contested proceedings Rust was found to be liable, PB would not, without more, be bound by that judgement, unless for instance it was a Part 20 Defendant or third party in such proceedings."*

This is rather more interesting: if party A indemnifies party B against a liability to C, even if C obtains judgment following a contested trial against party B, the principle of issue estoppel will prevent that judgment having the effect of establishing a liability on party A under its indemnity in favour of party B. If this is correct, it drives a coach and horses through what most people would see as the great advantage of having an indemnity in the first place. If the indemnified fights and loses a complex and expensive defence against a third party and then claims under the indemnity, this conclusion would mean that it would have to prove the liability all over again when claiming under that indemnity. However, this is arguably what Akenhead J decided – subject to the caveat that, if an estoppel could be established as against PB (the indemnifier), then PB could be estopped from arguing that the consent judgment was not proof of liability under its indemnity in favour of Rust.

This estoppel point went for consideration by Edwards-Stuart J ([2011] EWHC 1622 (TCC)). He in turn also considered a large number of old cases dealing with indemnities. His judgment was that PB was not estopped as, for the estoppel to apply, Rust would have to show that PB, as the indemnifier, had acted in the knowledge or expectation of a claim being made against Rust. On the evidence, it had not: it had acted so as to minimise the possibility of the group's insurers getting involved and thereby causing additional cost and expense.

At this point, before we come to consider the judgment of the Court of Appeal, the course of the litigation will probably strike those readers who have struggled on this far as being frankly bizarre. The whole point of an indemnity against a third party liability is, the reader will think, precisely so that the matter does not have to be re-litigated and liability established afresh under the indemnity. Again, if it came down to estoppel, the indemnifier would be well advised to steer well clear of anything to do with the third party claim. We shall see presently whether these propositions survived the analysis of the Court of Appeal.

At the moment, let us note that the authorities relied on by PB were arguably to the opposite effect. Some old authorities at least tended to show, at least on one reading, that, unless the indemnifier was in some way put on notice of the third party litigation with some sort of indication that the indemnifier would be bound by the result, then the result of the trial between the third party and the indemnified would not bind the indemnifier. The indemnified would, in fact, have to go through the whole job of proving the underlying liability to the third party so as to make the indemnifier liable under the indemnity. Of course, there would then be all the attendant risk of inconsistent decisions being reached by different tribunals: the indemnified might find himself liable to the third party in one set of proceedings but unable to recover under the indemnity in another set of proceedings against the indemnifier.

Overall, the old authorities do not support such an extreme position. In *Parker v Lewis* (1872-3) LR 8 Ch App 1035, Mellish LJ opined that the position was that an indemnified facing a third party claim could give notice to the indemnifier to allow the latter to defend the action but, if the indemnifier refused to do so, then the indemnified could defend and settle the third party claim on the best possible terms and then claim that sum under the indemnity. As we have seen, this is the position represented in cases such as *Comyn Ching v Oriental Tube* and *General Feeds v Slobodna* considered immediately above. But Mellish LJ went on to say,

> "... *On the other hand, if he[19] does not choose to trust the other person with the defence to the action, he may, if he pleases, go on and defend it, and then, if the verdict is obtained against him, and judgment signed upon it, I agree that at law that judgment, in the case of express contract of indemnity is conclusive. ...*"

Mellish LJ went on to say,

> "... *it would be very hard, indeed, if, when he [i.e. the indemnified] came to claim the indemnity, the person against whom he claimed it could fight the question over again, and run the chance of whether a second jury would take a different view and give an opposite verdict to the first. ...*"

It is important to note that Mellish LJ stated this explicitly not as a statement of law, but rather as a point of construction: it would be unusual to construe an indemnity to bear such a meaning. This leaves

---

[19] There was some dispute in *Rust v PB Limited* as to which party this "he" referred to: Stuart-Edwards J held that it must refer to the indemnified, not the indemnifier.

open that the indemnity could be construed that other way – which was the point of the judgment before Akenhead J in *Rust Consulting v PB Limited*.

To some extent, the law was beset with a certain degree of uncertainty following these and other cases. The matter again came up fairly recently in *Ben Shipping Co (PTE) v An Bord Bainne* [1986] 2 All ER 177. As in *Parker v Lewis*, the facts are rather complicated and should not detain us. There was alleged to be an implied indemnity given by the charterer of a vessel in favour of the shipowner. Bingham J found that no such implied indemnity existed but he made some helpful observations *obiter* on whether there was some principle of law to the effect that giving notice to the indemnifier of the third party claim in some way "bound" the indemnifier to accept the result of proceedings determining the third party's claim. As he said,

> " ... *It is of course good sense and common practice for a defendant to give notice of a claim against him and any proposed settlement to a person against whom he intends to seek indemnity or contribution, if such person is not joined as a third party. This gives that person the opportunity to raise any points or objections he wishes, and will make it somewhat harder for him to raise arguments later which he could have raised at the time. It is, however, a large stride from a commonsense tactical practice to a rule of law ... The rule contended for would present the charterers with a choice between taking over the defence of the claim which they believe to be nothing to do with them and thereafter (if that belief was falsified) finding themselves bound to indemnify the shipowners against settlement of a claim even*

though the claim could be shown to be ill-founded or the settlement unreasonable. ..."

With all this by way of background, let us see what happened in *Rust Consulting* in the Court of Appeal ([2011] EWCA Civ 899 and [2012] EWCA Civ 1070), though we are only concerned with the second of these judgments.

As with all indemnities, it came down ultimately to the precise drafting. The judgment is brief and entirely shorn of citation of the old authorities which so weighed with the judges at first instance. In a sense, this shows the development of the modern law's approach to indemnities: rather than rely on authorities to give us a template approach to the application of an indemnity, it comes down to a matter of construction of the indemnity in question.

The Court of Appeal disagreed with Akenhead J at first instance and relied on the wording of the indemnity as well as the consequences of separating out well-founded liabilities from bad ones: according to PB Group's arguments, the indemnity would bite if Rust fought a case and won but not if it fought a case and lost.

On the contrary, the Court of Appeal found that the wording was sufficient to include

> *"bona fide settlements of claims, sums reasonably incurred in the defence of claims, whether successfully or unsuccessfully defended".*

Of course, there might be an argument about whether or not a particular settlement was reasonable and we have looked at some of the case-law on this point above. However, the Court of Appeal reverted to the peculiar facts of this case, namely, that PB Group had instructed Rust to consent to judgment for its own reasons relating to its insurance position and that there was no other authority dealing with precisely these unique facts. That being so, there was no reason to displace the ordinary conclusion that a judgment was final on its facts, and the fact of its being obtained by consent for the PB Group's own internal commercial considerations did nothing to alter that. The indemnity would be enforced.

Practice points

There are probably many indemnifiers who give an indemnity against a liability to a third party who might be surprised (even shocked) that the indemnified could simply consent to judgment and then claim under the indemnity for the whole sum. To be fair, this is not going to happen frequently, as the facts of *Rust Consulting* are somewhat extreme and the case was ultimately decided on the wording of the indemnity in question. There is probably a feeling that the indemnified should at the very least put up something of a fight and come to the best settlement reasonably available in the circumstances, as happened in *Comyn Ching v Oriental Tube*. This also raises the question of whether an indemnified should do anything to mitigate loss, which we shall look at shortly.

A similar point of course came up in *AXA v Genworth Financial International* [2019] EWHC 3376 (Comm), which we have referred several times already, where again recourse was had to old authorities to try to show that the cases on indemnities imported some sort of obligation on the indemnified to run reasonable defences before a claim could be made under the indemnity. It will be recalled that the court instead preferred to construe the words of the contract itself rather than approach the wording with any predetermined notions as to what the consequences should be.

In truth, there is no binding authority on the point: some of the older authorities are not reported well and the *ratio* is unclear while the more recent authorities tend to focus on the exact wording of the indemnity without recourse to authority for guidance (other than ordinary rules of construction). If an indemnifier is providing an indemnity to an indemnified against a liability to a third party, it would be advisable to set out in writing exactly how that liability should be established and setting out the respective obligations of the parties including a consideration of at least the following points:

- Notice of third party claim by indemnified to indemnifier (and its status as condition precedent to liability under the indemnity or otherwise)

- How the third party claim should be handled and by whom (indemnifier or indemnified)

- A description of what a "liability" is – is it a well-founded claim claim (only) or is a claim that has a reasonable chance of success?

- If it is a claim that has a reasonable chance of success, who makes that call?

- Who determines what is a reasonable settlement, who conducts the negotiations, who has the right to authorise or veto a settlement?

What is a "claim"?

Finally, for completeness, some consideration should be given to this point. As with all cases on indemnities, it will come down the precise wording of the indemnity. While there may be some argument over whether "liability" means a judicially established liability or just a potential liability, a claim may be for a something that is ultimately upheld at trial, or it may be a weak claim that can possibly be disposed of in a summary trial – it may even be a claim brought by a third party who is a complete crank or a vexatious litigant and which is absolutely hopeless. What does it mean to give an indemnity against a "claim"?

There is little authority on the point in the context of indemnities, but some guidance can be got from *Codemasters Software v Automobile Club de l'Ouest* [2009] EWHC 2361 (Ch). The case will be discussed in the next section, but (briefly) Automobile Club de l'Ouest (ACO) was the provider of an indemnity to Codemasters in respect of certain images of racing cars for use in promoting a computer game. The indemnity was,

> *"... from any and all claims, causes of action, suits, damages or demands whatsoever, arising out of any breach or alleged breach of any agreement or warranty made by the indemnifying Party pursuant to this Agreement."*

There are obvious problems with this indemnity's wording, one of which is what was the meaning of "alleged breach"? Did it cover a mere allegation or did that allegation have to have at least some substance? Did it in fact mean that the alleged breach had to be established by a judgment upholding the "alleged breach"?

As with all indemnity cases, the decision is based on the precise wording. As Arnold J put it, in dealing with the argument that "alleged breach" must mean "a breach which was presently alleged and, in due course, established",

> *"In my judgment, that is an untenable interpretation of the words 'alleged breach' since it effectively reduces those words to the same meaning as 'breach'."*

It is worth dealing with the problem of what happens in the context of a "claim" – after all, a claim could sit anywhere on a spectrum from a well-founded claim to a ridiculous claim brought by a vexatious litigant that has zero chance of success. Would such a claim even qualify as a "claim": all would depend on the precise wording of the indemnity.

In *Ben Shipping v An Bord Bainne (The C Joyce)* [1986] 2 All ER 177, which we considered above, the owners of the vessel "C Joyce" paid out against claims brought by cargo owners and then claimed an indemnity from the charterers (ultimately unsuccessfully). The owners gave notice to the charterers of the claim, and invited the charterers to take over the conduct of the defence. As we have seen, this is not normally an incident of being an indemnifier without express words to that effect and, in any case, the charterers (indemnifiers) refused to have anything to do with the claim. As the court observed, serving notice put the indemnifier in something of a dilemma and it rejected the idea of serving notice as a prerequisite to recovery under an indemnity,

> *"... [T]he rule contended for would present the charterers with a choice between taking over the defence of a claim which they believed to be nothing to do with them and thereafter (if that belief was falsified) finding themselves bound to indemnify the*

> *owners against settlement of a claim even though the claim could*
> *be shown to be ill-founded or the settlement unreasonable. ..."*

The effect of the judgment was that the charterers were not estopped from denying the validity of the judgment and were therefore still able to contend that the cargo owner's claim was not valid and that the vessel owner's compromise of the claim was not a proper and reasonable one. Many commercial lawyers will say that including an indemnity will lead to swift and uncomplicated settlements of claims, but this case should stand as a warning: unless some wording is included to compel the indemnifier to intervene, then the indemnifier could well stand back and continue to dispute the applicability of the indemnity to the claim that has been made and then to dispute the reasonableness of the settlement reached by the indemnified.

Practice point

When you provide an indemnity against "claims" or "alleged breaches", what exactly are you offering? Are you really providing a complete indemnity against any claim, even ones that are completely hopeless claims put up by vexatious litigants in the hope of a quick payment? While each indemnity will be read according to its own wording in its own context, this may well be the effect.

In that case, providing for an indemnity against a liability may well be a narrower indemnity, since it would import some element of reasonableness in disposing of the claim, which would in turn import some consideration of the strength of the claim. Giving an indemnity against just an alleged breach may well be something wider than just a breach – it is up to you as the one drafting the indemnity.

Are some things irrecoverable under an indemnity?

One point that is often included in an indemnity is an obligation to indemnify in respect of any fines or penalties that are imposed on the indemnified as a consequence of any breach of contract (or other duty) by the indemnifier. Say the indemnifier is providing outsourced IT services to the indemnified and, in the course of doing so, causes the indemnified to be fined for data protection breaches by the Information Commissioner's Office. Many indemnities in such contracts provide for the IT service provider to indemnify the customer against any liability in the nature of penalties or fines.

It seems clear from the insurance sector that insurance cannot be provided against criminal liabilities: if an insured has an insurance policy in respect of a car, the insurer cannot be made to pay any fines imposed by the courts for careless or drunken driving. This raises the question of whether an indemnity could possibly cover administrative fines imposed by a regulatory body falling short of a criminal punishment.

There is no case directly on the point as far as the writer knows but *Safeway Stores v Twigger* [2010] EWCA Civ 1472 may cast some light on the issue. It concerned a claim for an indemnity as a legal remedy, not a claim under a contractual indemnity as such, but it is instructive nonetheless.

The defendants were senior executives and directors of Safeway, a leading retailer, who had surreptitiously engaged in price fixing arrangements to help to increase the price of milk, thereby causing Safeway to infringe the Competition Act 1998. Following Safeway's takeover by Morrisons, the Office of Fair Trading launched an inquiry and indicated that it would be imposing a penalty on Safeway. Safeway, under its new owners, claimed indemnity from the defendants for any penalty that might be imposed as a consequence of their breach of contract and/or fiduciary duty. Safeway also claimed as damages the costs of meeting the OFT's investigation, amounting to some £200,000.

The defendants sought summary judgment, saying that Safeway could not recover these sums from them, relying on the old maxim of *ex turpi causa non oritur actio*. At first instance, the judge accepted that the provisions of the Competition Act were sufficiently illegal or unlawful so as to engage the maxim and that a penalty under the Competition Act was akin to a fine, but sent the matter for a full trial. The defendants appealed, claiming summary judgment to dismiss the claims against them.

The Court of Appeal reviewed the history of the maxim and its status in the current law: in essence, it existed to ensure that the criminal and civil courts spoke with one voice. If a criminal court imposed a fine on a person, that person could not go to a civil court and effectively transfer the liability for the fine to a third party. In this case, the liability was imposed directly on Safeway by the Competition Act: this much derived from the Act itself, which only allowed a fine where Safeway had "intentionally or negligently" committed the infringement. There was no liability under the Act on the defendants themselves. It was this direct imposition of liability on Safeway which was decisive: otherwise, it would be arguably correct that the acts of the defendants (as agents of the company) could not be attributed to Safeway as they were in breach of their duty to their principal and had resulted in harm to that principal. The Court of Appeal therefore allowed the defendants' appeal and gave summary judgment in their favour.

While not directly on the point, this decision is of great value as a starting point. Of course, one feature of *Safeway Stores* is that the defendants were private individuals and the court may have had some sympathy for their personal plight in facing this claim brought by their former employer. Going back to the IT outsourcing example given above, if indeed the provider caused the customer to fall foul of data protection laws and thereby incur a fine imposed by the Information Commissioner's Office, the maxim could well apply to prevent recovery under any indemnity in the contract. The legislation imposes a direct liability on the controller of the personal data, similar to the situation in *Safeway Stores*. A further feature is that the typical IT outsourcing contract would (doubtless) be replete with provisions relating to governance, reporting and auditing, so that it would be harder for the customer (indemnified) to argue that it was kept in the dark about the provider's (indemnifier's) possibly illegal activities. If there is some sort of no fault liability, then the answer could be different: for an example in the insurance field, see *Osman v Moss* [1970] 1 Lloyds Rep 313.

However, before it should be thought that *Safeway Stores* provides a clear answer to the problem, Pill LJ in a concurring judgment said this,

> *"On the present statutory scheme, the answer is in my view clear but other situations may be more complex. ..."*

In other words, different regulatory regimes and different factual scenarios may give rise to different conclusions. An indemnity against fines or penalties could, or could not, be enforceable.

CHAPTER FOUR
SCOPE OF THE
INDEMNITY

"... the word 'indemnity' may refer to all loss suffered which is attributable to a specified cause, whether or not it was in the reasonable contemplation of the parties. There is precious little authority to support such a meaning, but I do not doubt that the word is often used in that sense."[20]

What must an indemnifier do?

This is an interesting question. It will be recalled from *Firma C-Trade* that an indemnity in English Law can be seen in the same way as an insurance contract of indemnity: it is normally seen as an obligation to pay unliquidated damages against the happening of a defined event. In the insurance context, the event will typically be something such as a fire or another unwanted calamitous event, while in the field of a commercial contract an indemnity will be sought against the happening of a different sort of defined event, such as the indemnifier's breach of contract or the making of a claim by a third party of infringement of intellectual property rights.

---

[20] *Total Transport Corp v Arcadia Petroleum (The Eurus)* [1998] 1 Lloyds Rep 351 (CA) *per* Staughton LJ

Once this is understood, it will be appreciated that how the indemnifier chooses to satisfy the indemnity is a matter for the indemnifier, subject to any specific wording in the contract. We have already seen in the discussion above concerning settlements, liabilities and claims, that an indemnifier may sit back and do nothing and simply pay (or perhaps more likely: dispute) the bill presented to it by the indemnified or it may come forward to offer to deal with e.g. the third party claim by itself. Indemnifier and indemnified may dispose of the matter by agreement as they please at any time, or they may set out in the indemnity clause itself a detailed conduct of indemnity provision describing precisely what each party is obliged to do following the triggering of the obligation to indemnify.

The situation can be compared with that in the insurance field. An insurer may offer the insured an indemnity against the losses consequent on the insured's suffering a burglary or a fire at his home. If either of these events occurs, then the insurer must pay compensation according to the terms of the policy (or otherwise as provided by the law of damages). However, without express words in the policy, the insurer is not obliged to install a burglar alarm or a sprinkler system at the insured's home, or to try to extinguish a blaze when it breaks out, nor must an insurer seek to apprehend the burglar as he leaves the insured's premises with his bag of swag swung over his shoulder.

This may come as a surprise to many lawyers in the commercial field, who assume that a contractual indemnity in and of itself obliges the indemnifier to step into the breach, leap to the defence of the indemnified and take on the trouble, cost and expense of, for example, dealing with and disposing of a third party claim within the terms of an indemnity. If that is the result desired, then the wording needs to be precise to achieve that result.

The point came up for (admittedly brief) consideration in *Codemasters Software v Automobile Club de l'Ouest* [2009] EWHC 2361 (Ch). Codemasters was a designer and seller of computer games and came to an agreement with Automobile Club de l'Ouest (ACO) which operated the well known "24 heures du Mans" motor car race as well as other, less gruelling, races around the world. The agreement was for the marketing of a game called "Race Driver Grid" which was envisaged as including various elements taken from the Le Mans race itself. By the agreement, Le Mans licensed various intellectual property rights for use in marketing the game, including representations of various racing cars used in the 2006 Le Mans competition. The agreement also provided,

> "*10.3. Each party (the 'Indemnifying Party') will indemnify, <u>defend</u> and hold harmless the other party and its affiliates, parent companies, subsidiaries, and their respective directors, officers and employees, from any and all claims, causes of action, suits, damages or demands whatsoever, arising out of any breach or alleged breach of any agreement or warranty made by the indemnifying Party pursuant to this Agreement.* "[emph added]

In this case, Codemasters used images of certain racing cars (including trademarks and designs) only to find themselves receiving claims from Ferrari, Lamborghini and Porsche to the effect that the use of those images was not authorised and that ACO had no right to authorise them.

What did it mean to "defend" – what obligations did it impose on the indemnifier or what rights did it give them? A point raised by ACO was that the inclusion of "defend" meant that Codemasters was obliged to entrust the defence of any claim to ACO. Arnold J disposed of this argument swiftly,

> *"In my judgment, that is not a tenable interpretation of clause 10.3. Read in context, while again it is not happily worded, it seems to me that the word 'defend' is being used merely in the rather general sense of 'protect from'. At most, it <u>may</u> give Codemasters, as the indemnified party, the right to request that ACO take over the defence of any proceedings brought against it. I do not consider that it can be interpreted as imposing upon the indemnified party a mandatory requirement to hand over the conduct of the defence of any claim to the indemnifying party."*
> [emphasis added]

It is of course open to the parties to include a conduct of indemnity provision to set out the steps each party is required to take on the happening of the event indemnified. These provisions are becoming common in commercial contracts and can now be quite complex: indeed, they have become for many lawyers and commercial parties what an "indemnity" is supposed to be, although strictly speaking, they are not the indemnity itself as that term is narrowly understood in cases such as *Firma C-Trade*. Typically, the indemnifier will wish to reserve to itself the sole right to conduct and pay for any defence of a claim made by a third party falling within the indemnity but the reason for this is typically the practical one that it wishes to ensure that it is the one paying the cheapest bills and making its own decisions about what the best compromise is of e.g. a third party claim.

The precise wording of an indemnity can be crucial: too many lawyers (and others) drafting indemnities simply pile up long lists of items (e.g.

"all losses, claims, demands, damages etc etc") without considering what each element means or what they mean when all taken together. Two cases show that express wording can, in context, have a different meaning from that which appears on paper.

In *Tesco Stores v Constable* [2008] EWCA Civ 362 Tesco constructed a supermarket on top of infill over a railway tunnel. The tunnel collapsed. As part of the agreement to carry out the works, Tesco had entered into a deed of covenant with Chiltern Railway in respect of certain costs, losses and expenses it might incur in the event of mishap. Tesco became liable to Chiltern under this deed. The question was whether it could recover this liability from its public liability insurers. The relevant words of the policy provided that the insurers would

> "... indemnify [Tesco] against all sums for which [Teco] shall be liable at law for damages ...".

Did this cover contractual liability under the deed of covenant? The Court of Appeal upheld the judge's decision that it did not: "all sums" was a broad term but in the context of a public liability policy the words should be construed to mean those sums which resulted from a liability to the public under actions in tort, not actions in contract for pure economic loss.

Another example can be seen in *Anglian Water Services v Crawshaw Robbins* [2001] BLR 173 where a subcontractor of Crawshaw Robbins, while working on Anglian's water mains, drilled into water and gas mains as well as severing electrical cables, having a serious effect on a fifth of Corby's population: local residents complained that water was actually coming out of their gas appliances. Anglian paid out various sums in order to put matters right, including making *ex gratia* payments to householders who had been affected. The contract provided at clause 22 that Crawshaw Robbins would

> *"indemnify and keep indemnified [Anglian] against all losses and claims for injuries or damage to any person or property whatsoever ... which may arise out of or in consequence of the construction and maintenance of the Works and against all claims demands proceedings damages costs charges and expenses whatsoever in respect thereof or in relation thereto."*

Stanley Burnton J had no doubt that "all losses" did not extend to *ex gratia* payments, and was intended only to cover legal liabilities:

> *"An indemnity clause is not normally used to extend the liabilities of the indemnifying party to sums paid by the other party without his having been under any legal obligation to do so. If that is to be its effect, clearer words, bringing the extended liability clearly to the attention of the indemnifier, are required."*

Conduct of indemnity clauses

While there is a deal of law on conduct of claims clauses in the insurance field (as may be expected), there is little as yet in the context of contractual indemnities. An old insurance example (but still vital in the modern law) can be seen in *Groom v. Crocker* [1939] 1 KB 194. William Groom was driving his brother, Aubrey, when his vehicle collided with a lorry owned by Tear Bros. Aubrey was injured and sued both Tear Bros and his brother, William. William was insured for the accident and his insurers instructed Crocker, a solicitor, to conduct the defence. Although the insurers and Crocker agreed with William that Tear Bros was solely responsible for the accident, William's insurers in fact came to a deal with Tear Bros' insurers to share William's liability to Aubrey. The upside for William's insurers was a favourable deal they managed to do with Tear Bros' insurers on a completely different and unrelated matter. William had nothing to do with this settlement and never consented to such a deal. Crocker implemented William's insurers' instructions, and admitted liability on William's behalf. William was not happy.

William sued Crocker for breach of contract, in tort and for libel. It was held that, while William's insurers had in the policy reserved the right for themselves to decide on the proper tactics to pursue and the conduct of the action, this was not an unfettered right. There were implied boundaries and limitations, and this was not a discretion that could be exercised arbitrarily. Lord Greene MR even likened what William's insurers had done to accepting a bribe from the lorry owner's insurers and it meant that they had failed to exercise their discretion properly.

Groom v Crocker has been cited with approval in cases in the insurance field since, notwithstanding its harsh language describing the actions of William's insurers. As Mance LJ put it in *Gan Insurance v Tai Ping Insurance* [2001] EWCA Civ 1047, after discussing *Groom v Crocker*, and while noting that William Groom was a private individual with personal interests at stake,

> *"I consider that reinsurers' power to act on behalf of and to bind insurers would be subject to similar limitations: it should, at the least, be exercised in good faith and in the common interest on the basis of the facts giving rise to the particular claim and not arbitrarily or with reference to considerations wholly extraneous to the subject-matter of the particular claim."*

However, when looking for cases in the contractual indemnity (non-insurance) field, they are hard to find. A recent example can be seen in *Minera Las Bambas v Glencore* [2018] EWHC 1658 (Comm), where Glencore had given a tax indemnity in favour of Minera following the sale of a mining business in Peru to Minera. When the Peruvian tax authorities assessed tax, Glencore implemented the conduct of indemnity provision at clause 12.5.1(iv),

> "... [Glencore] shall be entitled at [its] own expense and in [its] absolute discretion, by notice in writing to [Minera], to take such action as it shall deem necessary to avoid, dispute, deny, defend, resist, appeal, compromise or contest the Third Party Claim (including making counterclaims or other claims against third parties) in the name of and on behalf of [Minera] ... "

This power vested in Glencore was subject to a proviso,

> "...provided that [Glencore] give notice to [Minera] and agree in writing to indemnify [Minera] against the full amount (if any) payable under such Third Party Claim (if adversely determined)... "

However, Moulder J found,

> "Accordingly I find that the purpose of the power to assume control of a claim under clause 12.5.1(iv) is to reduce/avoid [Minera's] liability to the third party and thereby to enable [Glencore] to protect themselves against being exposed to a claim under the indemnity given to [Minera] pursuant to the SPA and the Deed of Indemnity but, subject to the express proviso given in clause 12.5.1(iv) itself, there is no limitation, express or implied,

on the exercise of those powers such that the power cannot be exercised to the detriment of [Minera]. This conclusion is consistent with the language of the agreements and given the scope of the indemnity from [Glencore] to [Minera] under clause 3.1 of the Deed of Indemnity (which I have held to extend to matters both pre-and post closing), consistent with commercial common sense."

This is a somewhat surprising conclusion given the line of authority in the insurance sphere as to how a defence may be conducted on behalf of an insured and the limits implied into an insurer's power to do so, which are generally interpreted as a discretion. There has of course been a burgeoning line of authority relating to the exercise of a discretion in business contracts following on from *Braganza v BP Shipping* [2015] UKSC 17 (and even before that) not to mention the emergence of an acceptance of an implied duty of good faith in some "relational" commercial contracts.

While it is correct that Glencore, as indemnifier, ultimately carried the responsibility for discharging any tax adjudged to be due under Peruvian law, Minera had (at least) some interest in ensuring that the indemnity would be carried out by Glencore in a way that did not reflect badly on it in its future relations with the Peruvian tax authorities, just as William Groom had an interest in defending his non-negligent driving record as against not only the world but also his injured brother. The power given to Glencore was expressed to be "absolute", but did it really mean that they could do a side-deal with the Peruvian tax authorities akin to the situation in *Groom v Crocker* or that, in a different non-tax situation, it could bring hopeless counterclaims on Minera's behalf against Minera's best customer in pursuance of its own commercial interests?

However, the case stands as an interesting, perhaps solitary, example of how the courts may approach the exercise of a conduct of indemnity power. It is suggested that the line of authority deriving from the insurance arena should be seen as a good guide when it comes to exercising a conduct of indemnity provision.

Practice point

It may strike many commercial lawyers (and their clients) as an unusual outcome that "defend" in *Codemasters* did not in fact mean "defend" as most lawyers and their clients would understand the word. As was pointed out at the very opening of this book, lawyers have been drafting indemnities for years by building up a congeries of expressions (such as "defend and hold harmless", "save and hold harmless" or "indemnify and keep indemnified") without realising that these expressions do not in reality have a universally agreed core meaning and that an indemnity is normally seen by the law as just an obligation to pay a sum of money by way of damages on the happening of a defined event.

When it comes to conduct of indemnity clauses, the drafting point is clear. If you wish to include a conduct of indemnity provision describing what each party is required to do when it comes to implementing an indemnity, then each party needs to look to see that its own interests are reflected in the wording. Is the right or power given to the indemnifier an unfettered power, such that the indemnifier could make admissions of liability on the indemnified's behalf, or is it a discretion and, if so, what are the factors limiting the exercise of that discretion?

What must an indemnified do?
The duty to mitigate loss (or not)

There is nothing in the general law binding an indemnified to do anything in particular. We have looked above at whether the law requires notice to be given by the indemnified to the indemnifier and concluded from the cases that, while there may be some tactical advantage in doing so, it is not a "legal" requirement (in the absence of any specific words to that effect in the indemnity clause itself).

This brings us to the vexed question of the applicability of the existence or absence of any "duty to mitigate" on the part of an indemnified.

Much has been made of the indemnified's duty to mitigate (or rather the absence of a duty to mitigate) and many commercial lawyers will cite this as the one great supposed advantage of an indemnity over a straight breach of warranty claim. The origin of this absence of a duty to mitigate in the modern law appears to derive from the decision of the Court of Appeal in *Royscot Commercial Leasing v Ismail* (29 April 1993, unreported). Let us take some examples of this use of *Royscot* in the modern law before looking at *Royscot* itself.

In *ABN Amro v McGinn* [2014] EWHC 1674 (Comm), McGinn had executed an indemnity in favour of ABN in support of a factoring agreement between ABN and Jenks Sales Brokers Limited, a company of which McGinn was a director. The indemnity was wide-ranging and indemnified ABN against all loss suffered by ABN in consequence of breaches of the factoring agreement. In fact, Jenks was in breach of that agreement by having records so poor that, when it went into administration, a specialist collections agency appointed by ABN was unable to recover more than about £5.5m leaving some £18.5m of outstanding debts, many disputed, allegedly owing to Jenks by its customers. The administrators admitted that some £8.9m was owing to ABN. McGinn argued that ABN had not done all it reasonably could to resolve those disputes and that most of the money could have been recovered from the recalcitrant former customers of Jenks.

One line of argument run by McGinn was that McGinn had failed to do what it reasonably could in order to recover debts from Jenks' customers such that it had caused its own loss or failed to exercise its duty to mitigate. This was given short shrift by Flaux J,

> "... Equally, failure to collect debts does not give rise to a defence of failure to mitigate under a contract of indemnity, as [counsel for McGinn] recognised: see the decision of the Court of Appeal in Royscot Commercial Leasing Ltd v Ismail (29 April 1993) and Codemasters Software v Automobile Club de L'Ouest [2009] EWHC 3194 (Ch); ... "

Another reference is made there to the *Codemasters* case, but this is a different judgement on different issues from that mentioned above. It will be recalled that the Automobile Club de l'Ouest (ACO) had given an indemnity in favour of Codemasters, a computer game manufacturer, which was said to be triggered when third party car manufacturers made claims of IPR infringement against Codemasters.

Turning to this particular judgment in the *Codemasters* litigation, it turned principally on the expert evidence required for a future full hearing on the question of quantum. ACO's expert had provided his opinion on various questions relating to, among other things, quantum and industry practice in the computer gaming world. Some of the matters on which he was required to express an opinion related to the reasonableness of certain actions that Codemasters could have taken to reduce or avert potential claims from third parties who had alleged infringement of their intellectual property.

After referring to various authorities including *Royscot*, Warren J said,

> *"The law, so far as I am concerned, is therefore that questions of mitigation do not arise under contracts of indemnity so as to give the indemnifier a defence to any part of a claim for which he would otherwise be liable under his indemnity. The line of authority considered is concerned with contractual indemnities. This should not be confused with a case where a claimant seeks to recover, as damages for breach of contract or in tort, his liability to a third party (whether as the result of a case taken to trial and judgment or as a result of a reasonable settlement). I see no reason why, in such a case, a defendant should not say that the liability (whether under the judgment or the settlement) should never have arisen but should have been reduced by reasonable steps in mitigation."*

From this passage, one can note immediately a slight (possible) inconsistency in approach: while there is (apparently) no duty to mitigate the scope or size of any matters within the indemnity, Warren J accepted the line of authority considered above when dealing with the settlement of liabilities (see the discussion above of *Comyn Ching v Oriental Tube* and other cases on this subject) but declined to extend it to cover other types of liability incurred within the scope of the indemnity.

One's eye therefore turns eagerly to the decision of the judgment of the Court of Appeal in *Royscot* itself as it is the *fons et origo* of the modern law's exclusion of any duty to mitigate on the part of an indemnified.

One expects expansive citation of authority by the Court of Appeal and a detailed consideration of the principles at stake so as to justify the absence of any duty to mitigate on the part of an indemnified. If one approaches *Royscot* with this expectation, one is going to be disappointed. It has never been reported in any series of law reports: it is a mere twelve pages long and mentions only a few cases before concluding that,

> *"... the rules of mitigation do not apply to a claim for debt due under a contract as contrasted with a claim for damages for breach of contract ..."*

The assumption underlying the case is that an indemnity is equated to a debt. However, it is by no means clear that this is correct. As Lord Goff put it in *Firma C-Trade v Newcastle P&I Club* [1991] 2 AC 1,

> *"... I accept that, at common law, a contract of indemnity gives rise to an action for unliquidated damages, arising from the failure of the indemnifier to prevent the indemnified person from suffering damage, for example, by having to pay a third party."*

However, a claim for unliquidated damages most certainly does come with a duty to mitigate loss. How can we reconcile these concepts?

Turning to *Royscot* itself, the facts concerned an agreement by which one Ismail indemnified Royscot, a financing company, in respect of a lease of equipment entered into by a company of which he was a director. The report is so brief that we do not even know what the equipment was. Be that as it may, the company breached (in some way – presumably by non-payment) the terms of the lease, leading to repossession of the goods and a claim under the indemnity against Ismail. The District Judge gave judgment for Royscot with damages to be assessed holding that there was an arguable case that Royscot had not mitigated its loss. The relevant parts of the indemnity read as follows,

> "I ... (b) agree upon written demand to indemnify you against all loss damage costs and expenses you may sustain ... (c) agree that the amount of your loss for the purpose of this Guarantee and Indemnity whether or not the Agreement shall have been terminated by any party thereto shall be the amount of the Lessee's liability under the Agreement plus all expenses you may incur in the exercise preservation or enforcement of your rights under the Agreement or in connection with any act done in or proceedings taken for the purpose of obtaining the return or possession of the goods from any person whatsoever ..."

It can be seen that this is a fairly clear statement of what sums Ismail would have to pay should he become liable under the indemnity. One possible *ratio* for this decision of the Court of Appeal is that, where a contract of indemnity provides very clearly for certain defined costs and expenses to be paid, then it is no defence to say that the indemnified has a duty to mitigate – the contract has provided for specific, precisely defined costs and expenses to be paid. After all, if I indemnify you against "all" costs and expenses, I can hardly turn round after the event and say, "but I didn't mean that expense".

The same principle can be seen in *McGinn*, discussed above. A further factor in the *McGinn* case was that ABN benefited from a conclusive evidence clause as follows,

> " For the purpose of determining my liability under this Indemnity I shall be bound by any acknowledgement or

> *admission by the Company and by any judgment in your favour*
> *against the Company. For such purpose and for determining*
> *either the amount payable to you by the Company or the amount*
> *of any losses, costs, damages claims (whether prospective or*
> *actual and whether as claimant or defendant) interest and*
> *expenses ("Losses") I shall accept and be bound by a certificate*
> *signed by any of your directors. In any proceedings such*
> *certificate shall be treated as conclusive evidence (except for*
> *manifest error) of the amounts so payable or of any Losses. In*
> *arriving at the amount payable to you by the Company you shall*
> *be entitled to take into account all liabilities (whether actual or*
> *contingent) and to make a reasonable estimate of any contingent*
> *liability."*

As with *Royscot*, the sums were therefore capable of very precise calculation just as in a debt claim – in fact, a certificate signed by a director of ABN would be conclusive evidence of the sum claimed (and the judgment contains a useful discussion of the cases on the meaning of this expression).

The Court of Appeal in *Royscot* considered the previous decision of the Court of Appeal in *Goulston Discount Company v Sims* [1967] III Solicitors Journal 670. In this case, a motor dealer, Sims, indemnified a finance company against certain losses suffered under a hire-purchase contract entered into with one Baylass. As with *Royscot*, the amount to be paid under the indemnity was precisely set out,

> *"[I]n consideration of your entering into a hire-purchase*
> *agreement with Mr R. Baylass [I] agree to indemnify you against*
> *any loss you may suffer by reason of the fact that the hirer under*
> *the said agreement for any cause whatsoever does not pay the*

amounts which he would if he completed his agreement by exercising the option to purchase. The date of loss shall be any date you notify us after termination of any of the said agreement or the hiring there under. Loss shall mean the difference between the total amount the hirer would have had to pay to acquire title to the goods under the hire-purchase agreement plus your expenses less payments received by you."

In fact, Baylass wrecked the car after making the first payment and failed to pay any further outstanding instalments. The car's value for insurance purposes had been given as £200, but for reasons described by the trial judge as Goulston's folly or recklessness, they only recovered £180 from the insurers.

The important point is this: Goulston calculated its loss as being the amount of outstanding installments minus £180. The Court of Appeal, in another strikingly brief judgment this time given by Lord Denning, disagreed: Goulston should make the calculation on the basis of the sum it should have received, namely, £200, not the £180 it had actually received.

The Court of Appeal in *Royscot* sought to distinguish this case, not altogether convincingly. Hirst LJ conceded that, "at first sight", Lord Denning's judgment "might possibly" be interpreted as referring to mitigation; however, he was "satisfied, considering the case as a whole" that the case turned on the precise words of the indemnity, not a statement of principle as to the general applicability of a duty to mitigate in the case of debt. It is curious to find two cases fairly close to each other in time, both in the leasing sector, with each deciding a similar point in two different ways. While one of them has been consistently followed, the other is barely mentioned in the case-law.

An interesting case looking at mitigation is *Scipion Active Trading v Vallis Group* [2020] EWHC 1451 (Comm). Scipion was a financing company that had security interests over stores of copper in Morocco, which Vallis was charged with storing and managing. For some unexplained reason, a large amount of copper went missing and Vallis admitted liability for the loss. Scipion claimed the value of the missing copper, but there was some copper still on site which could be sold. Vallis alleged that Scipion had failed to mitigate its loss by accepting one or other of various offers it had received.

The indemnity in the agreement read,

> *"7.1(b) [Vallis] shall indemnify SCIPION and keep SCIPION fully indemnified against all losses, damages, liabilities, costs (including all legal costs on a solicitors-and-clients' basis) and/or expenses of any nature whatsoever, howsoever incurred or sustained by SCIPION arising out of or in connection with any default by [Vallis] in either failing to provide the services in conformity with the provisions of [the CMA]..."*

A point initially taken by Scipion was that the various cases we have examined above (*Royscot, ABN Amro* and *Codemasters*) all meant that the indemnity should be treated as a debt and so without a duty to mitigate. For some reason, Scipion abandoned this argument at trial but instead argued that the wording of the indemnity should be read as being very wide and not importing a strong causal connection between the breach and the losses incurred. Scipion argued that its behaviour would have to be "highly egregious" or involve a "high degree of unreasonableness" before the indemnity became inapplicable.

The judge, in common with all modern indemnity cases, looked at the words themselves rather than talking conceptually about whether or not a duty to mitigate did or did not apply. He accepted that the rules on the duty to mitigate should be seen as an aspect of causation. He went on to hold that the words of the indemnity did indeed require some causal connection and rejected Scipion's arguments that would have given it a wide latitude as to how to behave following the breach. He therefore did examine the reasonableness of Scipion's behaviour and found on the facts that it had behaved reasonably such that it had discharged any duty to mitigate. The losses therefore were within the scope of the indemnity. Out of a very long judgment, the consideration given to the law in this area and the wording of the indemnity occupies a very small part. It achieves a sort of duty to mitigate, but does so by reading the very words of the indemnity themselves. One should not therefore leap to the conclusion that there is now a duty to mitigate in the context of ordinary indemnities.

Perhaps another sign that mitigation in the context of indemnities might just be an aspect of causation or remoteness could be seen in *AXA v Genworth Financial* [2020] EWHC 2024 (Comm). Clause 18.5 of the SPA in that case concerned the grossing up of payments made against any tax deduction or withholding:

> "*18.5 If any sum payable by a party under this Agreement ... shall be subject to Taxation in the hands of the receiving party, the paying party shall be under the same obligation, as under clause 18.4 above, to pay an additional amount in relation to that Taxation as if the liability were a deduction [or] withholding required by law.*"

This is a fairly common grossing up provision, but the judge observed that the intention was that the receiving party (AXA) should be "made whole" in the sense of not being out of pocket, so the clause in a sense operated as an indemnity, perhaps a quasi-indemnity. One point was whether AXA, as the receiving party, should be under some sort of obligation to use reasonable endeavours to minimise its tax liability in order to keep the grossing up obligation as low as possible. Bryan J declined to deal with this aspect in the abstract, preferring to wait until some real sums fell for consideration. However, he indicated that an implied term would not be the preferred route, but he would rather apply principles of remoteness or causation. It is an interesting thought, but the point did not arise for detailed consideration in that case, and it exists as a possible confirmation of the court's approach in Scipion above.

Let me now try to draw some loose strands together.

On the one hand, we have the established principle that there is no duty to mitigate in the case of a debt – this is of course correct. It has never been the case that an action for the price of goods sold is subject to some duty to mitigate on the seller's part. It might be subject to a counterclaim for damages for defects found in the goods after delivery, but that is very different.

However, we have other authority, at the highest level in the House of Lords (*Firma C-Trade*), to the effect that the action for breach of a contract of indemnity is an action for unliquidated damages.

It may well be that the equating of a debt to an indemnity was misplaced: perhaps it would have been better to liken an indemnity to a liquidated damages provision, where the amount of loss is fixed and cannot be mitigated. However, the case-law is what it is: I would suggest that there is a distinction between an indemnity setting out the scope of recovery in debt-like (or liquidated) terms and an indemnity where the precise amount is not easily ascertainable (for example, going beyond an arithmetical calculation based on a given formula e.g. an indemnity against a liability to a third party). Let us consider some examples.

Example One. You live in Newcastle and I promise to drive you to London to attend a meeting. I give you a contractual indemnity against your first class rail travel expenses to London if I fail to appear with my car at the agreed time to collect you. I fail to appear. You purchase a first class rail ticket. I would suggest that a court would be extremely unreceptive to my argument that you should have mitigated your loss by taking the coach instead. I have promised you one specific thing, and you are entitled to that thing. You are entitled to that thing because it falls directly within the scope of the indemnity. In that sense, the situation is like *Royscot* and *McGinn.* It does not matter for this purpose whether you regard the claim for the cost of first class rail travel as a debt, liquidated damages or as the correct measure of your loss in a claim for unliquidated damages: they all come to the same thing in this instance.

Example Two. You live in Newcastle and I promise to drive you to London to attend a meeting. I give you a contractual indemnity against your travel expenses if I fail to appear with my car at the agreed time to collect you. I fail to appear. "Great", you think, and order a stretch limousine and have yourself driven to London from Newcastle while all the time consuming the champagne you find in the limo's fridge. You present me with a bill for £1,000 and claim it as your travel expenses under the indemnity. I would suggest that a court would have great sympathy for my argument that the proper construction of "travel expenses" was "reasonable travel expenses for the likes of you and me".

It does not matter whether it is a debt or a claim for unliquidated damages: what does matter (as always) is the proper construction of the indemnity.

Example Three. You live in Newcastle and I promise to drive you to London to attend a meeting. I give you a contractual indemnity against your first class rail travel expenses to London if I fail to appear with my car at the agreed time to collect you. Three months before that agreed time, I repudiate the contract and refuse to drive you. You could, as is well known, at that stage go to an online ticket service and buy an advance first class ticket for £50, but in fact you wait until the day of travel and buy a first class ticket for £250 at the station. You claim this as the sum due under the indemnity. This is rather harder. The Court of Appeal in *Goulston* evidently had sympathy for the defendant in this sort of scenario: why in that case should Sims pay for the folly of the finance company in not seeking full recovery under the car insurance? Having said which, on a straight reading of the words, you are entitled to the full £250. It comes down again to a point of construction: a court might construe the indemnity as meaning that you will take such reasonable steps as to secure the cheapest possible first class ticket. In this way, it may be that a court in such a case would achieve in an indemnity case by a point of construction what the application of the duty to mitigate would achieve in a claim for unliquidated damages. It comes to the same thing, though the route is different. Having said all of which, nearly all recent judgments in this area such as *McGinn* show that the judges are not willing to look for a construction of the indemnity that would restrict the indemnified's right to full recovery under it. The exception to this is the very recent case of *Scipion Active Trading v Vallis Group* [2020] EWHC 1451 (Comm) which we considered above: the judge might well have regard to the very specific wording of the indemnity and then go on to assess whether the loss was the consequence of my breach. If that is correct, the judge might well say that the loss flowing from my anticipatory breach was the £50 you should reasonably have incurred rather than the £250 you actually incurred. This is, however, speculation: there is no "law" in this area mandating one or other conclusion and it would all depend on the wording of the indemnity – and the mood of the judge deciding the case on the day.

There are, in reality, too few indemnity cases in the modern law where the duty to mitigate has been properly considered in context rather than a simple citation of *Royscot* which is itself a case short of consideration of principle and rather dubious when seen alongside *Goulston* (to which it is close in time). This is probably a polite way of saying that *Royscot* is wrong as a basis for saying that there is no duty to mitigate in an action brought on an indemnity.

As was suggested above, we could perhaps make a distinction between those indemnities providing for a specific (or perhaps easily ascertainable) sum, akin to a debt, and those indemnities providing for the payment of amounts where the indemnified has a choice to make from within a range of possible expenditure. This would accord with the principle we have already seen in the cases concerning settlements of third party claims: the indemnified cannot simply pay a third party claimant whatever it demands and then seek full reimbursement under an indemnity (unless it is so worded to allow that level of recovery).

Under the present law, it is worth noting in passing that there is an inconsistency of principle here: to claim under an indemnity against third party liabilities, an indemnified must show that it was reasonable to settle and that the settlement was reasonable: see *Comyn Ching v Oriental Tube* (1979) 17 BLR 47 (CA) applying the well established principle in

Biggin v Permanite [1951] 2 K.B. 314. As we saw, there is a degree of latitude given to the indemnified in reaching a compromise but there is still a test of reasonableness before the amount can be recovered under an indemnity. However, to claim under an indemnity against costs and expenses, the indemnified can apparently incur as much as it likes without any concern that it should minimise them: see *ABN Amro v McGinn* [2014] EWHC 1674 (Comm).

At the moment, there is no consistency between the relatively few cases on contractual indemnities in the modern law which consider the point and the above is offered as a possible view. However, note that the courts at the moment simply tend to apply *Royscot* without the critical attention it perhaps deserves.

Practice points

This part of any indemnity strikes at the heart of what an indemnity might possibly cover – what an indemnifier might eventually have to pay (or do). Those drafting or agreeing to accept indemnities must understand that the law is currently short of consistent principle in this area.

The drafting points are therefore clear:

- Precision must be taken in describing the scope of the indemnity: take the examples above, instead of just "travel expenses", an alternative formulation could be given such as "reasonable travel expenses" or a precise formula such as "travel expenses up to the value of £50"

- Where there is the possibility of the indemnified under any particular indemnity having a range of options from which to choose in terms of incurring losses within the indemnity, then the scope of the discretion and the factors to be taken into account should be specified

- Moreover, words could be included providing that the indemnified should take reasonable steps to minimise or avert any claim under the indemnity akin to a duty to mitigate in a claim for unliquidated damages

- Following *Scipion Active Trading v Vallis Group* [2020] EWHC 1451 (Comm), it might be thought wise to set out that only losses claimable under the indemnity are those which flow directly from the breach that triggered the indemnity – see the next section on causation

- Of course, in a true duty to mitigate, a claimant can claim for the costs of steps taken which ultimately did not have the effect of minimising or arverting loss: whether this would be recoverable under an indemnity would come down to the precise wording – again, an indemnified would want to include some such words, while an indemnifier would likely not

Of course, if some sort of duty to mitigate a claim under an indemnity is inserted in the drafting, the indemnified might well ask what the point was of an indemnity over and above a straight breach of contract claim. Indeed, as we shall see shortly, there are other grounds for saying that a claim under an indemnity can in fact be somewhat narrower than a claim for breach of contract.

The law on mitigation of loss arose because of the recognition by the law that a victim of breach of contract could not simply sit back and let his losses accumulate, all the time safe in the knowledge that full recovery could be made from the hapless contract breaker. The duty to mitigate became part of the law of contract damages precisely to recognise and encourage reasonable behaviour – even on the part of a victim of breach of contract. If there is indeed no duty to mitigate on the part of an indemnified, then any requirement by an indemnified for an unqualified indemnity in a contract is in reality a claim for a licence to behave unreasonably. For this reason if for no other, the present ubiquity of indemnities in modern commercial contracts is a strange phenomenon.

Causation and remoteness

The linking words

In any indemnity, there obviously has to be some sort of connection between the loss which is incurred and the act triggering the indemnity. Again, it comes down to the precise wording, but some general points can be made.

In calculating contractual damages, regard is commonly had to the three great concepts of causation, remoteness and mitigation. These act as natural limitations on the recoverability of damages for breach of contract and exist independently of any contractual caps or exclusions. There are numerous authorities in the textbooks to give us guidance on how the law will be applied and what arguments can be adduced for either party.

When drafting an ordinary contractual warranty, it is like sailing along a known coastline, with principles of causation, remoteness and mitigation taking the role of lighthouses to serve as navigational aids. When drafting an indemnity, however, there is nothing like this at all: to draft an indemnity is to set sail on a sea littered with the flotsam of individual cases with no connecting principle to join them together.

This might be seen as one of the disadvantages of an indemnity: when advising on causation, remoteness and mitigation in an action for damages for breach of contract, the principles are well known and some advice can be given to the client on how things will likely play out at trial. When advising on the sums that might be recovered under an indemnity, there are no principles, only disparate individual cases which depend in turn on the general rules of construction as applied to the specific wording of the indemnity. What follows is a summary of some disparate cases, mostly to illustrate the problem, not to resolve it.

Causation – some examples of connecting words

In looking at indemnities quoted in the cases we have already considered, we have already quoted some formulations e.g.

- "... *any loss you may suffer <u>by reason of the fact that</u> the hirer under the said agreement for any cause whatsoever does not pay the amounts ...*"[emph added] – *Goulston Discount Company v Sims* [1967] 111 Solicitors Journal 670

- "... <u>*following and arising out of*</u> *claims or complaints registered with the FSA, the Financial Services Ombudsman or any other Authority ...*" [emph added] – *Wood v Capita Insurance Services* [2017] UKSC 24

- "... *in any manner <u>based upon, occasioned by or attributable to</u> the execution of these presents ...*" [emph added] – *Canada Steamship v The King* [1952] AC 192

Different formulae – and any review of the cases (or any review of contracts in commercial practice) shows a multiplicity of formulations. Does it make any difference?

At heart, English Law lacks a coherent theory of causation, simply providing practical solutions to the wording chosen by the parties in individual cases. In other words, there is no consistency running through the cases, nothing like a sliding scale of causation depending on the particular words appearing in the contract (with the possible exception of one case a little further on).

Some examples might make this clear. When reading the older cases, it should be borne in mind that the influence of *contra proferentem* and *Canada Steamship* are ever present: as has been stated above, these are influences with far less weight for the modern court in construing indemnities.

In *the Lindenhall* [1945] P 8 (CA), the defendant was the port authority of a port which suffered an air raid. It negligently decided to tow the Lindenhall through the harbour when she damaged by a mine. The contract provided,

> *"The owner or owners .... of the vessel .... being towed .... agree to indemnify and hold harmless the Port Authority against all claims for or in respect of loss of life, or injury to person or loss or damage of any kind whatsoever and <u>howsoever or wheresoever arising in the course of and in connexion with the towage.</u>"* [emph added]

The Court of Appeal came to a pragmatic decision: the wording did not cover damage caused negligently, this could not be said to be damage suffered *"in connexion with the towage"*.

In *Great Western Railway v Durnford & Son* (1928) 44 TLR 415 (HL), Durnfords took a lease of land from the GWR and a supplement to that agreement provided that Durnfords could use a portable gangway over the railway sidings on which a lorry could tip loads into wagons waiting in the sidings below. The agreement provided,

> *""... [Durnfords] hereby agree and undertake to indemnify [GWR] against all claims and demands or liability whatsoever whether in respect of damage to person or property <u>arising out of or in connection with the existence or user of the said gangway</u> ... "* [emph added]

In fact, an engine driver employed by GWR shunted a wagon so fast that it knocked a lorry off the gangway. The House of Lords was presented with a conundrum: the words were about as wide as they could be and on their face capable of covering what had happened. The result would be that Durnfords would be indemnifying GWR against its own employees' negligence. The result was that the words were read as being limited to Durnfords' acts, and not covering GWR's own negligence. This reflected what the House of Lords took to be the business purpose of the clause – that GWR should not be troubled by claims from Durnfords, not that it would be getting an insurance policy for absolutely anything that might go wrong.

Again, in *John Lee & Son v Railway Executive* [1949] 2 All ER 581 (CA) the Railway Executive leased a warehouse in the middle of railway sidings to Lee, where he stored goods. The contract provided,

> *""10. [Lee] shall be responsible for and shall release and indemnify [GWR] ... from and against all liability for personal injury (whether fatal or otherwise) loss of or damage to property and any other loss damage costs and expenses however caused or incurred (whether by the negligent act of [GWR] or their servants or agents or not) which <u>but for the tenancy hereby created or anything done pursuant to the provisions hereof would not have arisen.</u> "*[emph added]

A steam train emitted a spark that caused a fire in the warehouse. Lee sued for the Railway Executive's negligence. As the Court of Appeal observed, the words were so wide that they could capture just about anything – even making Lee indemnify the Railway Executive for a passenger being injured on the way to see Lee at the warehouse. The Court of Appeal declined to give the words such a wide meaning: they were intended to cover only those liabilities which arose as a result of the relationship of landlord and tenant, not more widely.

Breaking the chain of causation

Almost every case on an indemnity will concern causation: either the events that have happened fall within the wording of the indemnity clause or they do not.

The pragmatic approach of the courts is illustrated by *Total Transport Corp v Arcadia Petroleum (The Eurus)* [1998] 1 Lloyds Rep 351 (CA), not strictly a case on an indemnity, as that word was not used in the relevant clause. Arcadia had chartered the "Eurus" on a voyage charterparty for the carriage of oil from Nigeria. Given that prices were decreasing in February, it was important for Arcadia to ensure that loading completed in February so that a bill of lading would not be presented for January at the higher amount. Notwithstanding Arcadia's instructions, the bill of lading was dated 31 January: because of a uniquely Nigerian practice, not known to the parties, the bill of lading was backdated as loading was completed before 8am on the first day of the month. The arbitrators found that the parties did not and could not foresee that this peculiarity would lead to the bill of lading being backdated.

The indemnity read,

> *"Owners shall be responsible for any time, costs, delays or loss suffered by Charterers due to failure to comply fully with Charterers voyage instructions. Owners shall be responsible for any time, costs, delay or loss associated with vessel loading cargo quantity in excess of voyage orders. Additionally, Charterers shall not be responsible for any deadfreight for Owner's failure to lift minimum quantity specified in voyage orders."*

The Court of Appeal did battle with the wording. The paragraph does not use the word "indemnity" and so one question is whether it was what this book calls a "quasi-indemnity". Alternatively, was it to be seen as a simple statement of liability importing ordinary contractual levels of damages? If it is seen as a quasi-indemnity, is it confined to reasonably foreseeable loss? Was the loss "caused" by the alleged breach?

As we shall see in the next section, the Court of Appeal decided that the loss claimed was too remote (which of itself disposed of the case) but it also decided that the loss was not "caused" by the alleged breach. The arbitrators had with "commendable scholarship" had regard to learned works on the question of causation. However, could a chain of causation be broken by a pre-existing circumstance, namely, the Nigerian 8am rule?

Logically, it could not but the Court of Appeal had no truck with the niceties: the question was to take a common sense view of the situation and ask whether in common sense the wrongful act was a cause of the Arcadia's loss, or whether something else was. For Sir John Balcombe, giving a concurring judgment, the absence of the word "indemnity" was important and he simply applied the words of the clause: for him, the crucial element was why this particular clause should give Arcadia a complete indemnity for this particular breach while other clauses in the contract did not give the same level of recovery? The Court of Appeal did not think it was relevant to characterise the clause as an indemnity and then to apply certain consequences in terms of enhanced recovery for Arcadia.

A more interesting and recent case is that of *ENE Kos 1 v Petroleo Brasileiro (No 2)* [2012] UKSC 17. Given the multiplicity of judgments given by the members of the Supreme Court, it is hard to form a consistent view of the overall effect of the case, Lord Mance giving a powerful dissenting opinion. The owners of the "Kos" chartered her to Petroleo Brasileiro, the contract providing that, if hire was not paid when due, the owners had the right to withdraw the vessel. In fact, Petroleo Brasileiro failed to make a payment when due and the owners withdrew the vessel but not before a cargo had been loaded on board. Petroleo Brasileiro agreed, after some discussion, to unload the cargo, but by then precious (and expensive) time had been lost – 2.64 days, to be precise, along with some bunkers. The contract provided,

> "The master (although appointed by owners) shall be under the orders and direction of charterers as regards employment of the vessel, agency or other arrangements. Bill[s] of lading are to be signed as charterers or their agents may direct, without prejudice

to this charter... charterers hereby indemnify owners against all consequences or liabilities that may arise from the master, charterers or their agents signing bills of lading or other documents, or from the master otherwise complying with charterers' or their agents' orders... "[emph added]

The issue was that there were two causes in play here: was the loss caused by the loading of the cargo or the withdrawal of the vessel? It is a typical causation point that English Law does not have the intellectual apparatus to deal with, insead resorting to pragmatic conclusions based on the facts. The difference of opinion between the justices shows the difficulties this can lead to.

In the courts below, Andrew Smith J allowed the claim for the service of the vessel and for bunkers consumed under the law of bailment while the Court of Appeal rejected the claim on any basis whatsoever. However, the majority view in the Supreme Court was that the indemnity's business purpose was to protect the vessel's owner against unforeseen circumstances outside the normal course of a charter. This meant that the owner's reasons for withdrawing the vessel were irrelevant, entitling them to the costs of the delay in unloading the cargo under the indemnity. The question, according to the majority, was whether what happened was an "effective" cause of the owner having to incur the costs of unloading, costs they had not expected to incur in a normal time charter. So the test was not a "but for" test, but rather an "effective" cause test. This in turn meant that the "effective" cause need not be the sole cause. This had the result that an indemnity covered an unusual, not a common or run of the mill, event, the opposite of the approach in considering causation in the context of breach of contract claims. In actions for breach of contract, it is the unusual events that are held to be too "remote".

Lord Clarke's judgment was illuminating in seeing terms such as "proximate", "dominant" and "direct" as misleading, suggesting that the search was for a cause that was most proximate in time or one that was the sole cause. According to him, causation had to be established on the facts, but it was necessary to bear in mind the context in which the question was asked.

Lord Mance's dissenting judgment shows perhaps the dilemma of indemnity law since, after lengthy citation of earlier judgments on the question of causation, he concluded that the authorities required some sort of "direct" or "unbroken" causal link. For him, the question was whether the owner's loss was *"caused by compliance with the time charterer's instructions"* and for him, the answer was in the negative. It was caused because the charter had been brought to an end and the owner was no longer obeying the charterer's instructions. The dilemma for indemnity law is that, despite earlier authorities on indemnities going back many years, the approach of the modern courts is focused on the exact wording seen in context, not to base a decision on some sort of template approach to construing and enforcing indemnities.

The question of concurrent causes crops up from time to time when construing indemnities. As Steyn LJ put it in *E E Caledonia v Orbit Valve* [1994] 1 WLR 1515 (considered above),

> *"... we are not concerned with the notions of causa sine qua non or other abstruse theories of causation. The law is concerned with practical affairs and takes a common sense view. ..."*

As shown in that case, the court very typically eschewed nice questions of causation in favour of the proper construction of the wording of the indemnity.

Another case occurring more recently where the courts had to grapple with whether an indemnity could stretch to cover concurrent causes arose out of the striking facts in *Capita v RFIB Group* [2015] EWCA Civ 1310, which will be considered in detail below dealing with the duration of an indemnity.

Looser wording on causation

English courts tend to dislike philosophical questions around causation and stick to applying established canons of construction to the words of the indemnity on the page in front of them. The matter arises not infrequently as the court has to decide whether the linking words included in the indemnity dealing with causation (e.g. "resulting from", "in connection with" and so on) cover the events that have happened. In *E E Caledonia v Orbit Valve* [1994] 1 WLR 1515, one Quinn, employed by Orbit, was contracted to overhaul some valves on the Piper Alpha. He did so and retired to the accommodation module to rest. One of Caledonia's employees negligently caused an explosion which killed Quinn, among many others. The indemnity in question covered death or injury,

> *"... resulting from or in any way connected with the performance of this [agreement]."*

One point taken by Orbit was that Quinn was not at the time engaged in the "performance" of the contract – he had completed his tasks for the day and was resting. The Court of Appeal made quick work of this argument: the contract contemplated that Quinn would have to remain on the platform for some ten days while he was performing his daily duties. It did not matter that he was off duty at the time of the explosion – for the Court of Appeal, Quinn's death "resulted from" performance of the contract and was "in connection with" such performance.

A similar point came up more recently in *Campbell v Conoco* [2002] EWCA Civ 704 which highlights a possible distinction between "resulting from" and "in connection with", a point of considerable importance for those drafting commercial agreements in general. The facts are complex. Shaun Campbell was employed by Salamis on a North Sea platform owned by Conoco. Amec was contracted to carry out works to commission the platform which in turn subcontracted work to Salamis. While Campbell was working, he was struck by the sudden venting of compressed air. This had nothing to do with his job, it was a fail-safe response to an error condition. This was crucial, as the relevant indemnity between the operators provided for indemnity,

> "*... as a result of or arising out of or <u>in connection with</u> the performance or non-performance of the Contract ...*" [emphasis added]

The accident had nothing to do with Campbell's job as it was a freak occurrence. The Court of Appeal noted that the words were wide and also noted – and this is the useful point for those drafting indemnities – that "in connection with" is probably the broadest formulation, being as wide a connecting link as one can commonly come across. So there was no need for a causal connection and there had only to be a "connection".

However, this conclusion is not inevitable for this formula. *Campbell* was distinguished recently in *Scipion Active Trading v Vallis Group* [2020]

EWHC 1451 (Comm). The indemnity in question used the formula *"... arising out of or in connection with ..."* but the judge declined to hold that use of this formula in this particular indemnity meant that the parties had abandoned any type of causal link between the breach alleged and the loss incurred in consequence. The question being asked in *Campbell* was different: the enquiry was simply whether Campbell's activities could be said to be "in connection with" the performance of the contract and they were. Campbell was carrying out his duties as per his contract. The question in *Scipion* was different: the enquiry was whether the losses realised were in consequence of Vallis' alleged breaches of contract and duty. As always with indemnities, there are no hard and fast rules, only the application by the courts of specific wording.

Remoteness

As stated above, there is no concept of "remoteness" in indemnity law, only the results of some cases which show an individual court's reluctance to stretch an indemnity to unreasonable lengths.

Take the case of *City of Manchester v Fram Gerrard* (1974) 6 BLR 70 (QB). Manchester engaged Fram Gerrard to build an abattoir and meat market. Some time later, meat stored there became contaminated and Manchester had to pay various third party claims resulting from damage to the meat. The reason for that was that a subcontractor's work had led to cracks in the floor which in turn meant that the premises were not waterproof, which in turn necessitated water sealant work some three years later carried out by a third party, Keroc. It was this sealant which had contaminated the meat. Manchester's claim was put in the alternative, one alternative being that the original work was defective so necessitating Keroc's work which was the cause of the contamination.

The indemnity provided,

> *""14(b) Injury to property. [Fram Gerrard] shall be liable for and shall indemnify [Manchester] against any loss, liability, claim or proceedings in respect of any injury or damage whatsoever to any property, real or personal, in so far as such injury or damage arises out of or in the course of, or by reason of, the execution of the works, and provided always that the same is <u>due to</u> any negligence, omission or default of the contractor, his servants or agents, or of any sub-contractor"* [emph added]

The judgment is complex looking at the detailed evidence and the various arguments deployed by Manchester. The judge found on the evidence that the cracks were not in fact a default of Fram Gerrard or of its subcontractors. Even if they were, the original cracks were, as the judge put it, a *causa sine qua non* not the *causa causans*. As always with indemnity cases, it comes down to the exact wording: while the original subcontractor might have exceeded the right bay sizes thus leading to cracking which then required waterproofing works, the ultimate damage to the meat could not be said to be "due to" the original works, which was the connection required by the indemnity.

Perhaps another brush with the concept of remoteness can be found in *Mediterranean Freight Services v BP Oil (The Fiona)* [1994] 2 Lloyds Rep 506 (CA). Mediterranean Freight was the owner of the Fiona, which had been converted to operate as a tanker, albeit with some outstanding operational problems. BP Oil chartered her to carry oil from Rotterdam to the USA. While being checked at the port of discharge, a tank exploded causing death and considerable damage. The owners sought to recover from BP Oil under the indemnity contained in the Hague-Visby Rules at Article IV Rule 6,

> "*Goods of an inflammable, explosive or dangerous nature to the shipment whereof the carrier, master or agent of the carrier has not consented with knowledge of their nature and character, may at any time before discharge be landed at any place, or destroyed or rendered innocuous by the carrier without compensation and* <u>*the shipper of such goods shall be liable for all damages and expenses directly or indirectly arising out of or resulting from such shipment.* ...</u>"[emphasis added]

The judge found as a fact that the dominant or most efficient cause of the explosion was the contamination of BP Oil's cargo by the residue left over from the previous cargo.

The Court of Appeal found that Article IV Rule 6 took effect as an indemnity, similar to what this book has described as a "quasi-indemnity". The use of the words "directly or indirectly" probably had the effect, according to the Court of Appeal, of ousting the common law rules of remoteness set out in *Hadley v Baxendale* [1854] EWHC Exch J70. The actual result was that the indemnity was not applicable following *Canada Steamship* principles, as the owner had not used due diligence to provide a seaworthy vessel in breach of Article III Rule 1 of the Hague-Visby Rules and so had been at fault, and therefore outside the scope of the "quasi-indemnity".

All indemnities in modern times, however, come down to a question of construction. Take the case of *Total Transport Corporation v Arcadia Petroleum* [1997] EWCA Civ 2754, whose facts were set out in the previous section on Causation.

After dealing with various authorities in the shipping sector, the Court of Appeal considered that,

> *"A claim for damages is subject to the ordinary rules of remoteness ... A claim for indemnity is not subject to the same rules, but there must be an unbroken chain of causation between the signing of the bill of lading and the loss.*
>
> *No authority is cited for the proposition that remoteness is always irrelevant to an indemnity obligation."*

It was held that the words did not entitle Arcadia to recover loss that was not within the reasonable contemplation of the parties. Again, there is no rule about this in indemnity "law", and the Court of Appeal applied (as best it could) the wording before it to the special facts of the case and declined to characterise the wording as an indemnity and then to apply certain legally mandated consequences.

However, more recently, in *Capita v RFIB Group* [2015] EWCA Civ 1310, a share purchase agreement included an indemnity *"from any liabilities costs claims demands or expenses which any of them may suffer or incur arising directly or indirectly from"* specified matters. The trial judge thought that "directly or indirectly" imported that losses were recoverable under both limbs of *Hadley v Baxendale*. The Court of Appeal did not deal directly with the point, but Henderson J, giving a judgment concurring with Longmore LJ, thought that the use of these words meant that the losses claimed *"fell squarely within the wording"* of the indemnity. Once again, the approach of the courts these days is to have regard to the words of the indemnity themselves, not to approach them by forcing them into pre-existing legal categories: this includes remoteness, so there is no standard approach taken by the courts to deciding this point when considering indemnities.

Practice points

Nothing shows up the uncertainty inherent in indemnities than a consideration of causation and remoteness. All comes down to the wording and then it is in the judge's hands (followed by the hands of the judges in the Court of Appeal and then the Supreme Court). There is little that can be said other than to look at the above cases and consider their wording and use wording which is as broad (if you are the indemnified) or as narrow (if you are the indemnifier) as you can.

Just to highlight a very few of the points from the above cases:

- "In connection with" may be the broadest formulation, one to be favoured by the indemnified and avoided by the indemnifier – *Campbell v Conoco* [2002] EWCA Civ 704 (but this is not inevitable, see *Scipion Active Trading v Vallis Group* [2020] EWHC 1451 (Comm)

- "Directly or indirectly" may oust considerations of remoteness completely, again a formulation to be favoured by the indemnified and avoided by the indemnifier – *Mediterranean Freight Services v BP Oil (The Fiona)* [1994] 2 Lloyds Rep 506 (CA)

- Indemnity drafting tends to break down when dealing with concurrent causes and expressions such as "due to" or "resulting from" may lead to uncertainty – *City of Manchester v Fram Gerrard* (1974) 6 BLR 70 (QB)

CHAPTER FIVE
LIABILITY ISSUES

"The liability either falls within the scope of the indemnity or it does not. The kind of loss for which indemnity was claimed fell within the indemnity simply because it was loss arising out of liability for death or injury in respect of the contractor's employees."[21]

All or nothing

An indemnity is an all or nothing remedy: the loss claimed under the indemnity either comes within the wording, or else there is no remedy at all. There is no *pro rata* award made under an indemnity for being, say, 50% deserving (unless the indemnity is worded to have that effect). There is no "loss of a chance" type of award of damages for being almost within the indemnity but not quite.

This is illustrated by *AMF International v Magnet Bowling* [1968] 1 WLR 1028 (QB). AMF made and installed bowling alley equipment. There was an agreement between it and Magnet to install such equipment at various bowling alley centres owned by Magnet. In this particular instance, Magnet raised a purchase order on AMF to install a bowling alley at a centre then being built by Trenthams in Barnsley. The

---

[21] Lord Hoffman in *Caledonia North Sea v British Telecommunications (The Piper Alpha)* [2002] UKHL 4

agreement between Trenthams and Magnet contained an indemnity clause in the following terms,

> "... (b) Injury to property. Except for such loss or damage by fire as is at the risk of the employer under clause 15 (b) (B) of these conditions [Trenthams] shall be liable for and shall indemnify [Magnet] against any loss, liability, claim or proceedings in respect of any injury or damage whatsoever to any property real or personal in so far as such injury or damage arises out of or in the course of or by reason of the execution of the works, and <u>provided always that the same is due to any negligence, omission or default of [Trenthams]</u>, his servants or agents or of any sub-contractor." [emph added]

AMF started work but some weeks later the centre was flooded by heavy rain and its equipment was badly damaged. In the subsequent proceedings, the judge found that both Trenthams and Magnet were liable under the Occupiers Liability Act: Trenthams' share was 60% and Magnet's was 40%. Magnet claimed that Trenthams was mostly responsible such that it was liable under the indemnity. Moccatta J rejected this,

> ""... I can see no grounds for holding 60 per cent. responsibility to be the effective cause and 40 per cent. only a sine qua non."

The general point of principle he expressed as follows,

> "In the indemnity cases the party giving the indemnity merely undertakes to pay the other party money in certain circumstances. If, as a matter of construction, the event that has

occurred falls outside those circumstances, no liability to indemnify arises."

Reference has already been made above to *Greenwich Millennium v Essex Services* [2014] EWCA Civ 960. This was the case where Robson had supplied labour only services to HSE for plumbing on two blocks of flats. That labour had created defective pipework which was visible on handover and acceptance but not picked up by HSE at the time. Considerable damage was caused when the pipework failed and caused extensive flooding damage. The indemnity provided,

> *""[Robson] hereby agrees to indemnify [HSE] against each and every liability which [HSE] may incur to any other person or persons and further to indemnify [HSE] in respect of any liability, loss, claim or proceedings of whatsoever nature such as shall arise by virtue of the breach or breaches of this Subcontract Agreement by, or act, default or negligence of [Robson]."*

As Jackson LJ observed,

> *"Finally I should add that counsel are agreed that apportionment between HSE and Robson is not possible. Therefore this is an all or nothing case. I agree with that analysis. Robson's liability to HSE is contractual."*

Reducing loss before payment under the indemnity

The case of *Ibrahim v Barclays Bank* [2012] EWCA Civ 640 is of some interest although the facts are extraordinarily complex. In any case, the standard rule for recovery under an indemnity is in all cases a question of construing the indemnity and making payment according to the words themselves.

The case concerned the possible sale of LDV, a Midlands based manufacturer of vans. LDV was in financial difficulties. While the UK Government did not want to fund LDV, it was reluctant to see it go under. A potential purchaser was Weststar, a Malaysian company controlled by Ibrahim. Against LDV's imminent demise, Weststar agreed to buy the shares of LDV from its owner, it being ultimately agreed that UBS in Singapore would provide a letter of credit in favour of the UK Government with Ibrahim providing an indemnity in favour of UBS. In fact, Weststar decided not to pursue its purchase during due diligence, meaning that LDV went into administration. LDV's bank, Barclays, claimed under a guarantee it had received from the UK Government, the UK Government then claimed this sum under the counter-indemnity given by LDV, and the UK Government also demanded payment under the letter of credit given by UBS, and Ibrahim was made to pay UBS under his indemnity in favour of UBS. As can be seen, Ibrahim was ultimately the loser financially in this complex and interlocking chain.

In case the above recitation of facts is too complex for easy comprehension, the bare essentials are that the UK Government claimed sums under a counter-indemnity from LDV, but received these sums from UBS under a letter of credit. Did the receipt of moneys under the letter of credit extinguish the UK Government's rights against LDV under the indemnity?

This was important for Ibrahim: he was the financial loser in all of this. If he could be subrogated to the UK Government's rights against LDV, then he could make a recovery using those subrogated rights. Were there any rights to which he could be subrogated?

In brief, the Court of Appeal concluded that the payment under the letter of credit extinguished the UK Government's rights under the counter-indemnity, meaning in turn that there was nothing for Ibrahim to be subrogated to. To come to its conclusion, the Court of Appeal had to go back to the eighteenth century, taking in judgments from the nineteenth and twentieth centuries as well. However, this was a case where UBS acted under compulsion – it had undertaken to make the payment under the letter of credit and so the old cases on agency and ratification did not apply. The letter of credit made it clear that UBS would, on payment, be covering the sums unpaid by LDV and so the payment of itself discharged whatever it was that LDV owed to the UK Government. Another argument used by Ibrahim was that the letter of credit itself functioned as an indemnity akin to an insurance policy, but the Court of Appeal swiftly disposed of this argument: an insurer or indemnifier is entitled to inquire into the actual loss suffered by the indemnified (or insured) whereas a letter of credit functions as an obligation to pay against satisfaction of the conditions for payment (normally, in international trade, the presentation of the correct documents).

All this is a lengthy demonstration that an indemnity will compensate for loss falling within its precise terms. Once there is no loss, as in this case because the UK Government (the indemnified) received payment of exactly what it was owed, there was no outstanding obligation left on the indemnifier's (LDV's) part and no further rights on the indemnified's (UK Government's) part, leaving Ibrahim with nothing to be subrogated to.

Reducing loss after payment under the indemnity

There is a shortage of authority here. One interesting, though old, case on the point is *Burnand v Rodocanachi* (1882) 7 App Cas 333 (HL) where Rodocanachi took out insurance policies with Burnand on a cargo, which was destroyed by a Confederate cruiser. Rodocanachi was paid money by the underwriters according to the insurance policy. Following the conclusion of the US Civil War, the US Government paid Rodocanachi the difference between the sum paid out under the insurance policy and the real value of the cargo as an *ex gratia* sum. Burnand claimed to be subrogated to Rodocanachi's rights and claimed this sum. The House of Lords rejected this claim: the sum paid by the US Government was not paid in compensation, rather it was in the nature of a gift. As Lord Blackburn put it,

> ""*[W]here there is a contract of indemnity (it matters not whether it is a marine policy, or a policy against fire on land, or any other contract of indemnity) and a loss happens, anything which reduces or diminishes the loss reduces or diminishes the amount which the indemnifier is bound to pay; and if the indemnifier has already paid it, then, if anything which diminishes the loss comes into the hands of the person to whom he has paid it, it becomes an equity that the person who has already paid the full indemnity is entitled to be recouped by having that amount back.*"

The case is of some antiquity: it is not known whether this principle has ever been applied successfully in a contractual indemnity case, but it may be of some vitality in the modern law in cases where an indemnified receives a payment under an indemnity and then receives a sum which reduces the loss claimed under the indemnity. This is relevant to insurance – see the discussion below. Perhaps the modern law would look on this as an example of unjust enrichment rather than the equity proposed by Lord Blackburn.

The effect of limiting liability under the indemnity

One question commonly asked is whether a cap on liability affects liability under an indemnity. Another one is whether a limit expressed as applying to the indemnity applies to a claim for breach of the indemnity or, perhaps more accurately, the terms providing for how the indemnity should be performed. This latter situation is illustrated by the rather extraordinary facts in *Muhammad Issa El Sheikh Ahmad v Ali* [1947] AC 414 (PC), a decision of the Privy Council on appeal from the Supreme Court of Palestine. While this can hardly be said to be a case of antiquity, it is still of some age, and the usual caveats should be entered as some different principles of construction were then applied to indemnities as has been explained above. Moreover, a decision of the Privy Council is of persuasive value in English Law and its consideration of the relevant local law, the Ottoman legal code, makes it a rather curious decision. However, its principle finding is probably correct and it is necessary to consider it.

The case concerned a contract for the sale of land to an initial purchaser which was not completed. There was a liquidated damages provision in favour of the first purchaser. For reasons which are not clear from the report, the land was never transferred to the first purchaser and the vendor entered into a second contract to sell the selfsame property to a second purchaser. The parties were aware of the risk of a claim from the first purchaser and there was inserted into the second contract the following provision,

> "3. In the event [the first purchaser] claims from [the vendor] the [purchase price] and the said liquidated damages, [the second purchaser] undertakes to guarantee and to pay all these amounts on behalf of [the vendor] on condition that they will not exceed the amount of £P.2017 excepting the expenses, costs and advocate's fees and provided that [the second purchaser] will have no right of recourse against [the vendor] for any part of the amounts as they form part of the consideration in accordance with their agreement from now."

Clause 7 also contained a detailed conduct of indemnity provision whereby the vendor had to notify the second purchaser if the first purchaser made a claim and allow the second purchaser to conduct and pay for the defence.

The land was transferred to the second purchaser, after which the first purchaser indeed claimed his money back together with the liquidated damages provided for in the first contract of sale. The vendor notified the second purchaser, who paid the legal fees associated with the defence of the first purchaser's claim against the vendor. The vendor lost. The first purchaser got an order for payment by instalments, but the second purchaser only paid the first instalment. The first purchaser then executed judgment against other property of the vendor, which was sold at a great undervalue in execution proceedings. Part of the vendor's claim for damages was the amount of the undervalue. This far exceeded the limit of the indemnity. Could the limit on the indemnity be effective? Was the sale of the property at an undervalue too remote to be claimed as damages?

The Privy Council held that the clause in the second contract was an agreement to indemnify the vendor:

> *"Their Lordships agree with the view expressed by the courts below that the contract is in substance a contract to indemnify. That contract might well be performed by satisfaction of [the first purchaser] otherwise than by payment of money, despite the dissent of [the vendor] from that method of performance. A contract to indemnify such as is here present ..., on breach, gives rise to a claim for unliquidated damages ..."*

According to the Privy Council, the loss claimed was not too remote as the second contract actually contemplated that the first purchaser might make a claim and provided a procedure for dealing with such a claim. Of great interest are the following words of Lord Uthwatt,

> *"Whether the contract be read as a contract to indemnify the vendors at all stages or as a contract to indemnify the vendors against the amounts due to [the first purchaser] with a right in the vendors to fight [the first purchaser] to such extent as they chose, the result is, in their Lordships' opinion, the same. In any event, the limit on the amount payable under the guarantee is irrelevant in measuring the damages for breach of it. On the first basis the damages claimed fall within the terms of the contract on its true construction, and on the second they are damages which, on the facts found by the trial judge, might reasonably be expected to be in the contemplation of the parties."* [emph added]

In other words, the claim for the breach of an indemnity is not a claim for debt but a claim for unliquidated damages, when ordinary contractual principles will apply. The fact that the indemnity is limited to a certain sum will not act as a limit to the damages that may be claimed for breach of it. The fact was that the second purchaser had simply not carried out his side of the bargain and seen to the satisfaction of the first purchaser by whatever means he chose – this was a simple breach of contract leading ultimately to the vendor being forced to sell property at an undervalue to satisfy the judgment obtained by the first purchaser. In the circumstances, this was not too remote and could be claimed as damages for breach of the indemnity notwithstanding that it far exceeded the limit on the indemnity itself.

We will come back to this curious decision a little later: is this conclusion correct when seen against a different legal principle, namely, that the proper remedy for the failure to pay damages is interest, not further damages?

Duration of liability under an indemnity

Indemnity drafting can have strange and unexpected effects, as illustrated by *Capita v RFIB Group* [2015] EWCA Civ 1310. CHBC, owned by RFIB Group, had been involved in providing pension management and advisory services to the Queen Elizabeth's Foundation for Disabled People. One Le Cras, employed by CHBC, was involved in advising the Foundation day to day on managing the pension scheme. The trustees of the Foundation wanted to make some amendments in order to reduce liabilities. Le Cras executed this instruction by announcing the amendments but he never went on to formalise them, leaving them legally ineffective. By law, changes could only be made prospectively, never retrospectively. RFIB Group sold shares in CHBC to Capita in April 2004. At the time of the sale to Capita, no-one except Le Cras knew about the failure to formalise the amendments: he had instructed solicitors just prior to completion of the sale to Capita to formalise the amendments but they had correctly advised him that this could not be done retrospectively. Following the sale, Le Cras continued to misrepresent the situation even though he knew the reality and he did not forward the advice he had received. As a result, the liabilities were not reduced and in fact losses to the Foundation continued to mount. As late as December 2004 (the sale was in April 2004) Le Cras was still misrepresenting that everything had been done properly.

In the SPA between RFIB Group and Capita, there was an indemnity,

> *"5.8 [RFIB] undertakes to indemnify and keep indemnified [Capita] … from any liabilities costs claims demands or expenses which [it] may suffer or incur arising directly or indirectly from …*
>
>> *5.8.5 any services or products supplied by [CHBC] or any advice provided by [CHBC] (or any of its employees or agents) <u>prior to the Transfer Date</u>.* "[emph added]

What did "prior to the Transfer Date" mean? For a commercial lawyer, it would appear that the clear intention was to provide for losses arising before the Transfer Date to lie with the vendor, while losses arising after the Transfer Date would lie with the purchaser. But how did this apply to the loss-causing activities of Le Cras who was misrepresenting matters on a continuing basis both before and after the Transfer Date? This meant that losses arising from misrepresentations made before the Transfer Date kept being incurred on a daily basis both before and after the Transfer Date.

In fact, the Foundation only found out about the reality of the situation in October 2007, when formal amendments were put in place some time later in July 2008. The liabilities of the pension scheme were much higher than they should have been: the amount was estimated at £4.2m and the claim was settled at a mediation for £3.85m (which was agreed by the parties to be a reasonable sum).

How did the indemnity apply to this unusual situation? The question was whether there was some sort of continuing duty on the part of CHBC such that a fresh cause of action arose with each passing day. The Court of Appeal decided that this was not the case: the continuing failure to remedy the situation caused by Le Cras' misrepresentations did not mean that liability kept rolling on. The result was that Capita could claim under the indemnity for losses caused by Le Cras' negligence occurring before the Transfer Date, but this liability came to an end with Le Cras' fresh misrepresentations in December 2004, after which Capita as the new employer of Le Cras took responsibility for his actions and the losses accruing from that date.

The case could also appear in Chapter Four in the section dealing with concurrent causes. Reference could also be made to the recent case of *Gwynt Y Môr v Gwynt Y Môr Offshore Wind Farm* [2020] EWHC 850 (Comm) discussed above. The reality is that any indemnity is applied according to its terms.

Practice points

The decision in the *RFIB* case will seem a strange result for the commercial lawyer. Like all indemnity cases of the modern era, it turns on the specific wording of the indemnity but in this case with an admixture of older authorities that the Court of Appeal found hard to disentangle.

However, just looking at the wording of the indemnity, for most commercial lawyers, the intention will appear tolerably plain: all losses incurred up to the Transfer Date would lie with RFIB Group while all losses incurred after that date would lie with Capita. This result was only achieved in the minority judgment of Gloster LJ. It must seem strange that the interpretation of this clause should be caught up with a detailed analysis of two disparate lines of authority at Court of Appeal level. The Court of Appeal preferred the one to the effect that one action can have continuing consequences until a fresh action becomes, in effect a fresh cause. In this way, Le Cras' new misrepresentations in the December following the Transfer Date became a concurrent cause and stopped the indemnity from having effect.

However, the drafting points are clear enough:

- If you want to ensure that an indemnity only applies to losses arising prior to a certain date but to exclude causes of action accruing before that date that cause losses to arise after that date, you need to say so in express words
- Anyone drafting an indemnity may wish to specify exactly which losses are included in the scope of the indemnity, such that the draft makes clear when the first date is that they arise and when they end (regardless of the time of the action causing the loss)

Does an indemnity act as the sole remedy?

A contract may well have an indemnity providing some sort of remedy for the indemnified and the indemnifier may seek to argue that the indemnity provides an exclusive remedy, ousting a claim for breach of contract. If that is the intended result, then the drafting would have to be precise to achieve that effect.

This argument was run in *Anglian Water v Crawshaw Robbins* [2001] BLR 173 where the judge said,

> "I have no doubt that [the indemnity provision] is not the exclusive remedy of the Employer in respect of his liabilities resulting from the Contractor's breach of contract. Far clearer words would be required to deprive the Employer of his normal claim for damages for breach of contract, on the principle of Mowbray v Merryweather [1895] 1 QB 640, in respect of such liabilities."

The same argument had been advanced in *AMF International v Magnet Bowling* [1968] 1 WLR 1028, and was rejected by Moccatta J:

> "I agree with Mr. Wallace that [the indemnity] cannot be construed as a kind of exceptions clause in favour of Trenthams, so as to prevent Magnet from being able to recover damages for breach of a contractual obligation by Trenthams if the indemnity provisions in that clause do not, on their true construction, apply to that breach."

Practice point

The moral is clear: if you include some sort of indemnity clause in a contract and intend it to be the sole remedy for the subject matter it covers, then express drafting is needed to achieve that effect. In fact, the consequence of including both an indemnity and other contractual obligations covering the same ground will be that the indemnified may well have claims under both heads, with possibly inconsistent results. This was acknowledged in *Anglian*, but the judge held that this was not a sufficient reason of itself to hold that the indemnity clause had in some way ousted an ordinary claim for breach of contract.

Liability clauses and indemnities

This is a much asked question but one to which there is no easy answer. As with any question about a contract, the correct answer will come down to the precise words used. The difficulty is, as the reader will have seen above in the discussion of the (absence of any) duty to mitigate, some cases have regarded an indemnity as being in effect a debt, so excluding any duty to mitigate. Thus, if a cap on liability is expressed as limiting a liability for <u>damages,</u> then it would appear, on this line of authority, that such a cap would not operate to limit liability under that indemnity. As against which, if an indemnity for a precise sum is regarded as a liquidated damages clause, as was suggested above, then the contractual cap might act as an upper limit on the sum recoverable under the indemnity or it might not, depending on the precise wording. On the other hand, if the indemnifier refuses to carry out an indemnity that required him to take positive steps e.g. to conduct the defence of a third party claim, then that refusal would be the breach of a contractual obligation and would, apparently, sound in unliquidated damages which could, in turn, be subject to a contractual limit or exclusion of liability, depending on the precise terms.

As opposed to which, following a different line of authority, if an indemnity is given against a defined event occurring (such as a third party claim), then the proper remedy is a claim for unliquidated damages. This much is clear from Lord Goff's speech in *Firma C-Trade v Newcastle P&I Club* [1991] 2 AC 1,

> "... I accept that, at common law, a contract of indemnity gives rise to an action for unliquidated damages, arising from the failure of the indemnifier to prevent the indemnified person from suffering damage, for example, by having to pay a third party. ..."

More recently, in the context of a contract of indemnity insurance in *Endurance Corporate Capital v Sartex Quilts & Textiles* [2020] EWCA Civ 308, Leggatt LJ said,

> "... in a case where (as here) an insurer has agreed to 'indemnify' the insured against loss or damage caused by an insured peril, the nature of the insurer's promise is that the insured will not suffer the specified loss or damage. The occurrence of such loss or damage is therefore a breach of contract which gives rise to a claim for damages: see *Firma C-Trade SA v Newcastle Protection and Indemnity Association* ('The Fanti' and 'The Padre Island') [1991] 2 AC 1, 35; *Ventouris v Mountain (The Italia Express (No 2))* [1992] 2 Lloyd's Rep 281, 292; *Sprung v Royal Insurance (UK) Ltd* [1997] CLC 70"

So we have here something of a conundrum. For the purposes of limitations and exclusions of liability, is a liability under an indemnity to be seen as a debt, liquidated damages or unliquidated damages? Perhaps there are different types of indemnities with different rules applying to each type?

In the context of indemnity insurance, the law is quite settled: the insurer's liability to the insured is one to hold the insured "harmless" against an insured event; if that event occurs, then, as we have seen from the quotation from *Endurance Corporate Capital* above, the courts interpret the insurer's obligation to hold the insured harmless as being, in effect, a fictional duty to ensure that the event should not happen. This is indeed a fiction: if the event insured against is a fire (as in *Endurance Corporate Capital*) there is no way that the insurer itself could have prevented it short of installing its own sprinkler system. The fiction simply means that the insurer comes under a liability to pay damages to the insured following an occurrence of the insured event.

A further point flows from this in the insurance context. The insurer's liability is to pay unliquidated damages based on the fiction described above. If the insurer does not pay the damages, that is a failure to pay damages, not a failure to pay a debt. It is a fairly well established rule of law (though not without its critics) that the failure to pay damages does not give rise to a separate cause of action for the losses consequent on not receiving the damages in a timely fashion – see, for example, *President of India v Lips Maritime* [1988] 1 AC 395 (HL). In that case, there was an obligation to pay demurrage for exceeding permitted lay days. The umpire awarded compensation to reflect the collapse of the exchange rate, meaning that the demurrage, when received, was worth considerably less than if it had been paid on time. The House of Lords disagreed, finding that demurrage was simply liquidated damages and it was not possible to award damages for the failure to receive damages on time:

> "There is no such thing as a cause of action in damages for late payment of damages. The only remedy which the law affords for delay in paying damages is the discretionary award of interest pursuant to statute."

This can be illustrated in the non-insurance context by *Mandrake Holdings v Countrywide Assured Group* [2005] EWCA Civ 840. The case centred around a share sale of a company by Countrywide to Mandrake. A review had been commenced by the Securities Investment Board into pension mis-selling by the company being sold: this review was being done in two phases, the first phase looking at egregious cases prior to the second phase, which would be conducted after the share sale to Mandrake. There was a separate deed containing a covenant by which Countrywide undertook to pay for the pension liability. The parties and the courts appear to have proceeded on the basis that this was an indemnity. The question arose of whether the covenant extended to the liabilities under the second phase or just to the first phase. An additional claim was made for losses consequent on the failure to make the payment, Mandrake saying that the failure to make the payment destroyed its chances of making a profitable onward sale of the company it had bought from Countrywide, causing a loss to it of £15.5m.

The decision of the Court of Appeal arose in the context of an application to amend to include such a claim. Given the authorities, counsel for Mandrake was forced to accept as a general principle of law that an award of unliquidated damages was not available for the breach of a contract of indemnity where the breach consisted of not paying the damages. The Court of Appeal proceeded to dispose of the appeal against the judge's refusal to permit the amendment by itself granting leave to amend. The Court of Appeal recognised that this was a controversial area of the law, and that the law in Scotland was different on this point. However, for present purposes, it would appear that the law is as stated above pending any review by the Supreme Court.

This rule of law is applicable to the failure to make a payment which is equated to damages: a claimant cannot get damages for not getting his damages or for getting his damages late. The compensation for this is interest. However, if an insurer under a contract of indemnity is liable itself to perform e.g. the works of reinstatement, then damages can possibly (it seems) be awarded for the consequences of a failure to proceed with that work. This can be seen from *AXA Insurance v Cunningham Lindsey United Kingdom* [2007] EWHC 3023 (TCC) where AXA was claiming against Cunningham Lindsey in respect of the latter's professional negligence in failing to see to reinstatement works following subsidence at the insured's house. Damages were awarded for the failure to make good progress with the works including in respect of, for example, the insured's inconvenience and distress.

The Privy Council's decision in *Muhammad Issa El Sheikh Ahmad v Ali* [1947] AC 414 (PC) should now be reconsidered in the light of these authorities. It will be recalled that this was the case where the second purchaser of a property indemnified the vendor against claims made by the disappointed first purchaser of the same property. The indemnifier did pay for legal fees but failed to satisfy the first purchaser leading to the first purchaser executing judgment on other property owned by the vendor. It was held that certain losses suffered by the indemnified, namely, the losses incurred on a sale by auction at an undervalue of other property in order to satisfy the first purchaser's claim, were recoverable under the indemnity. The Privy Council made the point,

> "... the limit on the amount payable under the guarantee is irrelevant in measuring the damages for breach of it."

The Privy Council had already observed that the breach of a contract of indemnity gave rise to a claim for unliquidated damages: if so, then the indemnifier's failure to pay those damages could not give rise to a further claim for damages as was illustrated in *Mandrake Holdings v Countrywide Assured Group* [2005] EWCA Civ 840 (see above). Perhaps the Privy Council approached the case on the basis that the indemnity was more than just an obligation to pay money and came with a duty to take positive steps to defend the claim brought by the first purchaser: if so, this might explain the decision, as damages can (apparently) be awarded for the indemnifier's failure to take positive steps under, for example, a conduct of indemnity provision, as was shown in the insurance arena by *AXA Insurance v Cunningham Lindsey United Kingdom* [2007] EWHC 3023 (TCC) (see above). All told, this is a confusing area and, given the doubts expressed by the Court of Appeal in *Mandrake Holdings* as to the principle that a claimant cannot get damages for the failure to receive damages (or to receive damages timeously), the law in this area should be regarded as unsettled.

Finally, in the context of liabilities, it is worth mentioning the judgment in *Caledonia North Sea v British Telecommunications (The Piper Alpha)* [2002] UKHL 4. This case also concerned the disastrous explosion and fire on the Piper Alpha, a rig operating in the North Sea, causing massive loss of life and injury to the workers on board. The estates and the injured threatened to bring their action in Texas where they would benefit from higher compensation than would be awarded in the Scottish courts. Settlement was reached at a level between what a Scottish court would have awarded and what a Texan court would have awarded. The operator of the rig sought to recover under the indemnity in its contract with the contractor. That contract provided,

"*21 Consequential loss*

Notwithstanding any other provision of this contract, in no event shall either the contractor or the company be liable to the other for any indirect or consequential losses suffered, including but not limited to, loss of use, loss of profits, loss of production or business interruption."

The contractor argued that the exclusion of consequential loss invoked the second limb of *Hadley v Baxendale* [1854] EWHC Exch J70[22] which meant that the higher level of settlement was not recoverable under the indemnity. Lord Hoffman stated,

"... Clause 21 limits the liability of the parties for losses caused by breach of contract. Certain kinds of loss are excluded. But this is not a claim for breach of contract. It is a claim to an indemnity for a liability incurred by the operator outside the contract. In my opinion clause 21 has no application to such a claim. The liability either falls within the scope of the indemnity or it does not. The kind of loss for which indemnity was claimed fell within the indemnity simply because it was loss arising out of liability for death or injury in respect of the contractor's employees. As for quantum, the Lord Ordinary's finding that it was reasonable to settle at the agreed level is sufficient to make the sums which were paid recoverable."

Let me try and draw some loose strands together. It will be immediately apparent that there are too few cases as of yet to be able to offer up a coherent "law of indemnities" in the context of liability provisions. As

---

[22] Whether this would be true according to modern canons of construction is debatable: see e.g. *Transocean Drilling v Providence Resources* [2016] EWCA Civ 372

we have seen, some cases appear to approach the issue by assuming that the indemnity provision, albeit a contractual stipulation whose breach sounds in unliquidated damages, is to be regarded as akin to a debt, even if it is not actually a debt under ordinary legal principles.

A different way of approaching the problem is suggested as follows. An indemnity provision, as the primary obligation, will cover all those sums within the scope of the indemnity as drafted. When construing the scope of that primary obligation represented by the indemnity, concepts like mitigation or remoteness are simply inapplicable. Similarly, an exclusion of consequential loss will not apply. s These consequences flow not because an indemnity is a debt, but because the only valid question is whether any given loss falls within the scope of the indemnity as drafted. However, the breach of an indemnity provision will lead to the secondary obligation to pay damages according to ordinary legal principles: it is at that point that the duty to mitigate and all the other points concerning the assessment of quantum of damages become relevant. However, those principles cannot work retrospectively to reduce the amount within the scope of the indemnity seen as a primary obligation, as the wording of the indemnity has already determined those losses.

Another way of looking at this conundrum was considered when discussing mitigation in the context of a claim under an indemnity, it was suggested that indemnities could be divided into two different categories: first, there is the "debt-like" or "liquidated damages" category where an indemnity simply reimburses a specific or perhaps easily ascertainable sum and, secondly, there is a larger category where an indemnity is promising to do something such as to undertake certain steps e.g. paying for and conducting the defence of a claim made by a third party. Of course, strictly speaking, this is arguably not an indemnity at all: an indemnity is an undertaking to be liable in unliquidated damages against the happening of an indemnified event which the indemnifier promises will not happen.

Many "indemnities" in modern commercial contracts, however, fall into this second category – indeed, most indemnities in modern commercial contracts seldom relate to the payment of fixed or easily ascertainable sums of money; rather, they offer an indemnity against the consequences of the indemnifier's breach of contract or against claims made by third parties. These are not indemnities to pay a fixed or easily ascertainable sum: whether the sum is easily ascertainable would be a question of construing the indemnity and applying it to the facts, a far cry from the relatively easy arithmetic apparently open to the Court of Appeal in *Royscot*.

Let us look at some examples with the caveat that no case actually deals explicitly with these situations as far as the writer is aware and everything would in any case depend on the precise wording used in the contracts concerned.

Example One. The indemnifier indemnifies the indemnified against defined costs and expenses which are easily ascertainable following the application of some simple arithmetic (as in *Royscot*). There is a limit of liability for damages for breach of contract by the indemnifier of £1m. The costs and expenses amount to £2m. If *Royscot* is right and this sort of indemnity is like a debt, then the indemnifier is liable to make the payment of £2m, unlimited by the cap on the liability for damages for breach of contract. On the other hand, if the court followed the line of authority to the effect that an indemnity sounds in unliquidated damages, then the limit of £1m would be effective as a cap on liability for the indemnity. If the indemnity is read as a separate obligation from the cap on damages, the indemnifier could be seen perhaps as an obligation to pay certain costs and expenses to which the cap does not, on its true construction, apply. Only the precise wording would make this clear.

Example Two. The indemnifier indemnifies the indemnified against a claim made by a third party for infringement of intellectual property rights. Such a claim is made. There is a separate liabilities clause providing for a limit of liability of £1m for any damages payable by the indemnifier. As we have seen, the indemnifier's liability is effectively to "hold the indemnified harmless" against such an event occurring and so the indemnifier comes under a liability to pay unliquidated damages if that event occurs. It would appear that the indemnifier's liability is limited in this case to the £1m. This assumes that the approach in *Firma C-Trade* is followed, and the liability under the indemnity should not be regarded as a debt, as has been suggested above.

Example Three. The indemnifier indemnifies the indemnified against all and any claims made by third parties for infringement of intellectual property rights. The contract goes on to provide that the indemnifier must itself see to and pay for the defence of any such claims if they occur. The contract in a separate liabilities provision limits the indemnifier's liability for breach of contract to £1m in the aggregate. Ten third parties appear each claiming £10m for infringement of intellectual property rights. It will cost £1m to defend each claim. Here is a problem: it will be cheaper for the indemnifier to refuse to defend any of them and simply offer to pay the £1m for breach of contract. Alternatively, the indemnifier could spend £1m on defending one of the claims and then refuse to do anything further. This would lead to the interesting question whether a deliberate breach fell within the limitation properly construed, a continuing and vexed problem. This approach is also subject to the possibility of the indemnified obtaining an order for specific performance in which case, the indemnifier would (it appears) have to conduct and pay for the defence of all ten actions, paying £10m in legal costs to defend all ten claims plus any damages, interest and costs awarded or the cost of any settlements.

The astute reader will have noticed that the obligation in the last example is not an indemnity at all as we have defined it following *Firma C-Trade*: an indemnity under English Law strictly so called is an secondary obligation to pay unliquidated damages on the happening of an indemnified event – the happening of the indemnified event is the breach of the primary obligation. Other than that obligation to pay damages, it is not an obligation to do anything in particular unless the contract provides otherwise.

The obligation of paying for and conducting a defence to a claim made by a third party of infringement of intellectual property rights is typically what people think of as an indemnity, but it is not strictly speaking an indemnity as such. Such an obligation may well be enforceable as an ordinary contractual obligation and, if breached, would be subject to either an award of damages or an order of specific performance, in which case ordinary rules of law will follow.

Practice points

It has to be said that there is no one case or body of case-law that makes all this clear. With the ubiquity of indemnity clauses, such cases are sure to appear soon which will clarify these points but, at the moment, there is little clarity. As with all indemnity drafting, precision in the wording is required.

Some suggestions for consideration in the drafting are as follows:

- Where the indemnity is for a specific or easily ascertainable sum, provide for a cap on that sum as well as providing for a cap on the liability for any breach of contract for the failure or delay in paying that sum

- Where the indemnity is for the occurrence of some event (such as a third party making a claim against the indemnified), make specific provision for the cap on the amount payable if such a claim is made including any failure or delay in paying that sum

- Where the indemnity provides for the indemnifier to perform some act or acts (such as paying for and conducting the defence of any claims made by third parties against the indemnified) make express provision for any cap on how much money is to be expended in performing those acts as well as for any failure or delay in performing them

In the last case, it will be advisable to provide for what happens after the cap has been reached: does the indemnifier simply down tools or is there to be some orderly handover of responsibility to the indemnified? Again, this points to the need for a detailed conduct of indemnity provision.

The interplay with liability provisions could have unintended consequences. Say an IT service provider agrees to provide an unlimited indemnity against security breaches. However, the liability clause provides that the provider's aggregate liability under the contract is £5m. A claim is made under the unlimited indemnity clause for £10m and is paid out by the provider. Depending on the precise wording, it may well be the case that the provider has exhausted the liability provision and is not liable for any other breaches of contract at all over the remainder of the lifetime of the contract.

Indemnities and insurance

Given that indemnities have much in common with contracts of indemnity in the insurance world, it is not surprising that any insurance provisions in a commercial contract containing an indemnity may well have some impact on the construction or application of the indemnity itself. As will be seen presently, this may be a point of construction, although there may in some cases be principles of law in play as well.

In *James Archdale v Comservices* [1954] 1 WLR 459 (CA), Archdales employed Comservices to redecorate its factory and other office premises. Comservices negligently caused fire damage to Archdales' buildings and machinery. The indemnity provision read,

> "*[Comservices] shall be liable for and shall indemnify [Archdales] against and ... shall insure against any liability, loss, claim or proceedings in respect of any injury or damage whatsoever to any property, real or personal, in so far as such injury or damage arises out of or in the course of or by reason of the execution of the works, and provided always that the same is due to any negligence, omission or default of [Comservices], ... and subject also as regards loss or damage by fire to the provisions contained in clause 15 of these conditions.*"

On reading the last phrase of this clause, the eye eagerly goes to clause 15 to see what it says:

> *"The existing structures and the works and unfixed materials (except plant, tools and equipment) shall be at the sole risk of [Archdales] as regards loss or damage by fire and [Archdales] shall maintain a proper policy of insurance against that risk, ... "*

How were these provisions to be read together? On the one hand, Archdales had to get its own fire insurance, but the indemnity did at first blush cover Comservices negligently causing fire damage. The Court of Appeal in fact decided that the indemnity provision covered negligence by Comservices but with a carve-out for fire damage, which was to be insured against by Archdales, which would take sole responsibility for loss or damage by fire, regardless of how (or by whom) it was caused.

As has been said in this book too many times already, it comes down to the proper construction of the words comprising the indemnity themselves. As Dillon LJ put it in *Surrey Heath v Lovell Construction* (1990) 48 BLR 108 (CA),

> *"The effect of the contractual agreement must always be a matter of construction ... It may be the true construction that a provision for insurance is to be taken as satisfying or curtailing a contractual obligation, or it may be the true construction that a contractual obligation is to be backed by insurance with the result that the contractual obligation stands or is enforceable even if for some reason the insurance fails or proves inadequate."*

The problem is that too many indemnity provisions are drafted without thought being given to how they are supposed to cohabit in the same contract with liability or insurance provisions. Having looked at *Archdale* above, we could now look at *Casson v Ostley* [2001] EWCA

Civ 1013, which is somewhat similar in its factual scenario, but with a different result.

Casson had bought a farm and wanted to renovate it, so employed Ostley to do the works including some plumbing. Casson had taken out insurance on the premises, but was underinsured as a result of an undervaluation by the estate agents. Ostley subcontracted the plumbing, in the course of which a fire started which caused significant damage. It was accepted that Ostley was negligent. But who was liable for the fire damage? The contract read,

> "15. ... works covered by ... this estimate, existing structures in which [Ostley] shall be working, and unfixed materials shall be at the <u>sole risk of [Casson] as regards loss or damage by fire and [Casson] shall maintain a proper policy of insurance against that risk in an adequate sum.</u> If any loss or damage affecting the works is so occasioned by fire, [Casson] shall pay to [Ostley] the full value of all work and materials then executed and delivered." [emph added]

> "16. [Casson] shall indemnify [Ostley] against all liability, loss, costs, claims or demands in respect of injury to persons and/or damage to property arising from any cause other than [Ostley's] negligence or that of [Ostley's] employees."

Perhaps surprisingly, the Court of Appeal, with maybe a feeling of sympathy for Casson as a private individual rather than a wealthy business, held that it was inherently improbable that a private individual would exempt a builder from its own negligence and held that clause 15 did not, in this case, have that effect. As Sedley LJ put it,

> *"... the words on the page make perfectly good sense in the defendant builder's favour; but if you apply them to his own negligent – or for that matter deliberate – acts they seem less sensible; so you ask whether the parties meant to go that far; before answering, you remind yourself that A does not ordinarily agree to absolve B from the consequences of B's own neglect or malice; you therefore look for words which make such absolution plain; and, finding none, you conclude that the words on the page do not mean what they say."*

The case appears to have proceeded on the then usual principles of applying *contra proferentem* and *Canada Steamship*: as we have seen, these are now of far less relevance in the modern law. Still, we have the decision in *Archdale*, when the same principles were routinely applied, but which comes to the opposite conclusion – and this where both contracts attributed the "sole risk" of fire damage to the employer.

At the risk of multiplying examples unnecessarily on this one point, it is worth mentioning *GD Construction v Scottish & Newcastle* [2003] EWCA Civ 16. Scottish & Newcastle were undertaking building works at a pub in Reading. It was assumed for the purposes of the preliminary issue to be decided in the case that a fire was negligently started by GD Construction. The relevant provisions were lengthy and complex, but the following features emerge:

- GD Construction indemnified Scottish & Newcastle against all damage done to property as long as it was caused by GD Construction's negligence

- This indemnity did not on its terms apply where damage was required to be insured against

- Scottish & Newcastle was obliged to take out joint names insurance for the buildings

In fact, Scottish & Newcastle did not take out any insurance policy at all so the buildings were uninsured against this particular risk. The Court of Appeal this time came to the same conclusion as in *Archdale* – the obligation on Scottish & Newcastle to take out insurance had the effect that GD Construction was not liable for the fire, even if caused by its own negligence. As Longmore LJ put it,

> *"... any building contract, which imposes an obligation on one of the parties to insure against the risk of fire, intends to require that party to insure against both fires caused by negligence of one of the parties and fires not so caused. That is what insuring against fire means, ... It does not mean that the party carrying out the insurance obligation must insure against some fires but need not insure against other fires."*

This is a very good way of putting the point: it is all the more surprising that a differently constituted Court of Appeal came to precisely the opposite conclusion in *Casson v Ostley*.

The mention of joint names insurance in the *Scottish & Newcastle* case leads to a consideration of some cases that have appeared dealing with this issue. The issue revolves around the right of subrogation: there may or may not be an express waiver of this right but for present purposes it should be noted that, if an insurer pays out to one co-insured, it may be prevented from proceeding against the other co-insured as there will be no right of subrogation in this situation deriving from the fact of there being joint names insurance.

This issue came up in *Co-operative Retail Services v Taylor Young* [2002] UKHL 17. Co-operative was having a new headquarters built at Rochdale when a fire broke out in 1995. This was followed by an avalanche of litigation between the various parties (employer, contractor, subcontractor, consultants and so on). Part of the case turned on a claim for contribution brought by architects and engineers, who were sued by Co-operative, against Taylor Young. To win, they needed to show that Taylor Young was liable under its contract with Co-operative.

The wording of the contract was lengthy and detailed, similar to the wording in *Archdale* considered above. By clause 20.2,

> *"The contractor shall, subject to clause 20.3 and, where applicable, clause 22C.1, be liable for, and shall indemnify the employer against, any expense, liability, loss, claim or proceedings in respect of any injury or damage whatsoever to any property real or personal in so far as such injury or damage arises out of or in the course of or by reason of the carrying out of the works, and to the extent that the same is due to any negligence, breach of statutory duty, omission or default of the contractor ..."*

However, the following clause 20.3 specifically excluded from this indemnity the property actually being worked on. Taylor Young was obliged to take out joint names insurance for the full reinstatement value of the work, which in fact it did. There were then detailed provisions prescribing how any insurance moneys received should be applied to the works of reinstatement, which Taylor Young again in fact carried out according to the terms of the contract.

The House of Lords had little else to do but to apply the literal words of the contract. Taylor Young could not be liable for any damages to the works being worked on – this liability was excluded by clause 20.3. The point of the insurance provisions was to ensure that any insurance moneys were applied to the work of reinstatement, regardless of how the fire was caused. Therefore, neither party could be liable to the other for the fire, as they had effectively excluded this risk by covering it by insurance. Taylor Young could be in breach of contract – but only if it had failed to take out the insurance or failed to carry out the works of reinstatement. The interesting point is that the House of Lords thought, without it being necessary for the decision, that having joint insurance would effectively mean that the parties could not be liable to each in contract, as it had the effect of excluding any right of subrogation by the insurers against either co-insured.

The issue is controversial – is it a rule of law or a point of construction? The matter came up for consideration in *Tyco Fire & Integrated Solutions v Rolls-Royce Motor Cars* [2008] EWCA Civ 286, another building case with insurance provisions coupled with an indemnity.

Tyco was providing a sprinkler system at Rolls-Royce's new manufacturing unit. A pipe burst causing a flood which damaged the works as well as other parts of the plant. It was assumed for the purposes of the case that Tyco was negligent. Tyco argued, among other things, that one joint named insured could not, as a matter of law, recover against the other. The Court of Appeal decided the case based on the construction of the indemnity in question, leaving open whether any such rule of law existed based on *Scottish & Newcastle* or otherwise.

Another issue arising with indemnities is what happens if a particular loss is covered by contractual insurance and by an indemnity: as between the insurer and the indemnifier, who is liable ultimately to pay? In *Caledonia North Sea v British Telecommunications (The Piper Alpha)*

[2002] UKHL 4, a employee of a contractor was killed in the Piper Alpha explosion, and the operator settled the claim brought by his executors. The insurers then brought a subrogated claim against the contractor relying on the indemnity in the contract between the contractor and the operator. The contractor's argument was to the effect that, if a contract had two indemnities, one of third party insurance and the other contractual, payment under either of them cancelled out the other, meaning that the insurers lost their right to be subrogated to the operator's claim against the contractor. This line of defence failed. As Lord Hoffman put it,

> "... I am of opinion that the indemnity under clause 15.1.c. was not secondary to or co-ordinate with any insurance that the operators might choose to obtain in respect of the same losses. I suppose that it would have been theoretically possible to frame the clause to confer an indemnity only insofar as the operator was unable to recover from its insurers, although one cannot imagine the parties in practice entering into such a contract. But this contract did not require the operator to take out any insurance at all. It therefore follows that the contractual indemnity was a primary liability and the underwriters were entitled to be subrogated.

The drafting point is obvious from what Lord Hoffman said: if you want to draft an indemnity that ceases to be operative after recovery from insurers in respect of the same loss, you can probably do so, but whether the parties would willingly enter into such a contract is open to question.

Practice points

This is a point that gets little attention from most commercial lawyers: often indemnities are scattered throughout a contract while in a separate clause there will be caps on liabilities and in yet another clause there will be provisions relating to insurance. These should not be treated as entirely independent matters as the consideration of the above cases shows that they are potentially closely linked:

- Subrogation apparently exists for contractual indemnities as much as for contracts of insurance: if you wish to exclude a right of recourse following recovery under a policy of insurance, this would need to be explicitly stated – *Caledonia North Sea v British Telecommunications (The Piper Alpha)* [2002] UKHL 4

- If you have provisions relating to insurance, then this may well have an effect on the construction or operation of any indemnities: the precise outcome would depend on the wording used in the contract, but the important point is that it should be considered

- If there is a provision for one of other party to take out joint names insurance covering some of the risk, there may or may not be a rule of law preventing recovery as between the parties following recovery under the insurance so it would be best to cover this point specifically in the drafting

CHAPTER SIX
HOW THE LAW APPLIES
TO DIFFERENT TYPES
OF INDEMNITY

"Why do draftsmen not take note of the impact of a clear and consistent line of judicial decisions?"[23]

Introduction

This brief final chapter will look at different types of indemnity in turn and will seek to illustrate how indemnities are applied by the courts in practice. The intention is not simply to repeat what has already been said, but to highlight some specific points that should be uppermost in the mind of the lawyer when drafting an indemnity of any of the following types. This chapter is not intended as an exhaustive list, only a guide to some salient points.

Indemnities are commonplace in commercial contracts these days but four principal uses of an indemnity can be identified:

---

[23] *Per* Steyn LJ in *E E Caledonia v Orbit Valve* [1994] 1 WLR 1515

1. An indemnity against non-performance (or defective performance) by a third party: commonly, this is the case with a parent company guarantee;

2. An indemnity against claims brought against the indemnified by a third party: this is commonly seen in IPR indemnities;

3. An indemnity against breach of contract or other wrongs by the indemnifier; and

4. An indemnity against claims made by the indemnifier: these are very common in the construction and engineering industries, where they are often in the form of mutual indemnities in respect of a defined type of loss, making them effectively an exclusion of liability for that defined loss.

Indemnity against non-performance by a third party

The commonest example is probably the parent company guarantee, but commercial contracts also include indemnities against defective performance by e.g. subcontractors. Typically, the parent company guarantee will include wording appropriate to both a guarantee and an indemnity. The reason for this is to circumvent any arguments around the validity of the guarantee: as we have seen in Chapter One, various legal arguments can be run to challenge the continuing validity of a guarantee and including both a guarantee and an indemnity is an attempt to get around this potential problem. If the guarantee fails, reliance can be placed on the indemnity instead.

The problem is that a guarantee and an indemnity are different beasts potentially offering completely different levels of compensation to the indemnified. This can be clearly seen in *Anglomar Shipping v Swan*

Hunter (The London Lion) [1980] 2 Lloyds Rep 456 (CA) where Anglomar was the UK subsidiary of a US parent company. Anglomar entered into a contract with Swan Hunter for the construction of a ship. Swan Hunter was itself the subsidiary of the second defendant in this case. As with most shipbuilding contracts, the provisions were lengthy and detailed, providing for a twelve month guarantee against defects in the vessel and also for an acceptance procedure leading to an acceptance certificate. Following acceptance and out of warranty, Anglomar sued both Swan Hunter under the shipbuilding contract and Swan Hunter's parent under the "letter of undertaking" provided with the original contract. Swan Hunter itself defended the action pointing to the contractual provisions and the fact that acceptance had taken place meaning that it had no further liability for defects in the vessel outside of the twelve month guarantee against defects.

However, Swan Hunter's parent had to defend the action based on the wording of its letter of undertaking, which read,

> *"We refer to the contract which is to be executed between yourselves and [Swan Hunter], and in consideration of your executing this contract we undertake that if [Swan Hunter] ... shall in any respect fail either to execute the Contract or commit any breach of its obligations, then we will indemnify you ... against all losses, damages, expenses or otherwise which you may incur by reason of any such default by [Swan Hunter] in performing and observing its obligations under the said contract."*

The question was whether Swan Hunter's parent could be held liable under its letter of undertaking when Swan Hunter itself could rely on the warranty and acceptance provisions as a complete defence to any liability.

The Court of Appeal noted that this was an indemnity, not a guarantee. The basic principle of a guarantee is that it is intended to be co-extensive with the underlying debt obligation – the guarantor only owes what the debtor owes. If the debtor is discharged, so is the guarantor: this is a basic principle of a guarantee flowing from the fact that it is a secondary liability. However, an indemnity is a primary liability and it would be applied according to its precise terms. Swan Hunter's parent had promised to be liable for *"all losses, damages, expenses"* following a default by Swan Hunter. It meant that Swan Hunter's parent could not rely on any defences available to Swan Hunter itself under the terms of the shipbuilding contract. Swan Hunter walked away free: its parent was found liable.

It can go further: one reason why the recipient of a guarantee will want an indemnity in addition is that the indemnity can be legally enforceable even where the guarantee is not. If the underlying debt obligation is not legally enforceable, then the indemnity, as a primary liability, could be enforceable even when the underlying debt is not. An example of this can be seen in the relatively old case of *Yeoman Credit Ltd v Latter* [1961] 1 WLR 828 where Yeoman, a finance company, provided a car on hire-purchase terms to an infant. Under legislation then current, this was an illegal contract and void as the hirer was an infant. The infant in fact paid nothing and Yeoman proceeded against the indemnifier, who had agreed,

> *"[t]o indemnify you against any loss resulting from or arising out of the agreement and to pay to you the amount of such loss on demand and whether or not at the time of demand you shall have exercised all or any of your remedies in respect of the hirer or the chattels but so that upon payment in full by me of my liabilities*

> *hereunder I shall obtain such of your rights as you may at your discretion assign to me.* "

As the Court of Appeal observed,

> "... *the object of the document appears on its face to be to protect the plaintiffs against loss — to see them harmless — rather than to make good the infant's liability ...* ".

The very fact that Yeoman wanted such compensation rather indicated that this was not a guarantee, as everyone involved in the underlying hire-purchase transaction was aware that the hirer was an infant thereby making the it void. The consequence was that this wording was an indemnity and was upheld as against the indemnifier, while nothing could be recovered from the infant himself as his contract was void for illegality.

Take another illustration. The debtor is in breach of contract to the tune of £1m. The contract between the debtor and the indemnified contains a limit of liability of £500,000. If the document is in fact a guarantee, the guarantor's liability is secondary – the guarantor becomes liable to pay what the debtor is obliged to pay but has not paid. The guarantor's liability would be a maximum of £500,000. However, if the relevant obligation were seen not as a guarantee but as an indemnity, then the result would depend on the precise wording. In principle, the indemnifier, having taken on a primary obligation, could be liable for the full £1m even though the debtor was only liable for only half of that sum.

This approach of including both a guarantee and an indemnity is fairly common with documents described as guarantees, but which are in reality indemnities. Take this wording from *McGuinness v Norwich &*

Peterborough Building Society [2011] EWCA Civ 1286, where clause 2.4 provided,

> *"As a separate obligation you agree to make good (in full) any losses or expenses that we may incur if the Borrower fails to pay any money owed to us, or fails to satisfy any other liabilities to us, or if we are unable to enforce any of the Borrower's obligations to us or they are not legally binding on the borrower (whatever the reason)."*

It is those final words which capture the point – the point is to make the indemnifier legally liable even if the underlying debtor is not. Note also the opening words, *"As a separate obligation ..."*: it is separate because the clause was not intended to be a guarantee, it was separate in the sense of being intended to be a primary obligation. As the Court of Appeal said,

> *"It is common ground that clause 2.4, which contains an indemnity in respect of loss and expenses caused by the borrower's default, creates a liability in damages."*

Recourse may be had to that case for an example of what can happen where the drafting confuses concepts of guarantee and indemnity: the document was headed "Guarantee and Indemnity" and indeed contained a guarantee at clause 2.2, whereas clause 2.4, as we have seen, was a "separate obligation" intended (presumably) as an indemnity, though it does not contain the word. As opposed to which, clause 4.2 talked about "your obligations under this Guarantee" as being those of principal, not just of surety. The lengthy judgment shows how confused drafting can give rise to many issues of law and construction. As was said in Chapter

One, the courts look at the substance, not the label, so a clause can talk about a "guarantee" yet be construed as an indemnity, and *vice-versa*.

Another problem that can arise with the enforcement of parent company guarantees/indemnities relates to the dispute resolution provisions in the various agreements. This is illustrated by *Alfred McAlpine Construction v Unex* (1994) 70 BLR 26 (CA) where Panatown employed McAlpine to construct an office building. Panatown's parent, Unex, provided a guarantee. Disputes arose under the construction contract and were referred to arbitration in accordance with its terms. However, in the course of the arbitration, McAlpine brought proceedings to enforce the parent company guarantee against Unex; in response, Unex applied for a stay of the court proceedings pending the conclusion of the arbitration. The terms of the indemnity were as follows,

> *"If Panatown (unless relieved from the performance by any clause of the Contract or by Statute or by the decision of a Tribunal of competent jurisdiction) shall in any respect fail to execute the contract or commits any breach of its obligations thereunder then Unex will indemnify McAlpine against all losses, damages, costs and expenses which may be incurred by McAlpine by reason of any default on the part of Panatown in performing and observing the agreements and provisions on its part contained in the contract PROVIDED ALWAYS that Unex shall not be under any greater liability to McAlpine than Panatown would have been liable in contract pursuant to the express terms of the contract."*

Here is the problem: two different dispute resolution tribunals charged with the same facts and the same contract. Could McAlpine continue with the court proceedings against Unex under the indemnity while the arbitration was pending with its subsidiary, Panatown, with the attendant risk that two different tribunals would come to two different conclusions?

The conclusion appears to be, Yes. The Court of Appeal was plainly troubled by this unusual situation and, as with any indemnity, tried to find the solution in the wording. As with *Anglomar*, this was construed as an indemnity, not a guarantee. As Evans LJ put it,

> *"Here, there is an hybrid situation, where the contractor/employer arbitration is pending. [McAlpine] cannot assert that [Panatown's] liability has been established, and he is entitled, in my judgment, to allege and prove what [Panatown's] liability "would have been", just as if no arbitration was in prospect."*

Glidewell LJ even thought that the liability under the indemnity might well be fixed by the result of the arbitration, but that McAlpine could still argue that it was not liable at all, or was liable for a different sum. In the light of the decision of the Court of Appeal in *Rust Consulting v PB Limited* [2012] EWCA Civ 1070, which was considered above in Chapter Three, this might or might not be correct.

The purview doctrine

It was stated in Chapter One that parent company guarantees frequently include both a guarantee and an indemnity so as to circumvent possible defences applicable to guarantees but not, apparently, indemnities (mention was made of the rule in *Holme v Brunskill* by way of example).

A further qualification exists in the so-called "purview" doctrine – the word "purview" deriving from a citation from the 1898 edition of Rowlatt's "Law of Principal and Surety" in *Triodos Bank v Dobbs* [2005] EWCA Civ 630 where the learned author stated,

> ". . . it is apprehended that assent, whether previous or subsequent to a variation, only renders the surety liable for the contract as varied, where it remains a contract within the general purview of the original guarantee . . . . If a new contract is to be secured there must be a new guarantee."

The court in *Triodos* noted that this principle was illustrated in the earlier case of *Trade Indemnity Co Ltd v Workington Harbour and Dock Board* [1937] AC 1.

Going back to *Triodos*, Dobbs had executed personal guarantees in favour of Triodos to guarantee two loan agreements between Triodos and a company of which Dobbs was a director. The facility was increased two years later from £800,000 to £1.98m but a further replacement agreement was made a year later raising the maximum facility to £2.6m. Even though the guarantee agreement was drafted so as to allow the maximum leeway to Triodos in making amendments to the loan agreements (to get around the rule in *Holme v Brunskill*), the Court of Appeal decided that the later replacement agreement was not within the "purview" of the original guarantee and could not be said to be a variation or amendment permitted by the terms of the guarantee but was rather a different agreement, and therefore outside the guarantee.

The decision in *Triodos* has not been without significant academic criticism. This was noted in *CIMC Raffles Offshore v Schahin* [2013] EWCA Civ 644 where a holding company provided a guarantee for sums due on delivery of two drilling rigs to subsidiary companies. The beneficiary of the guarantee was the builder of the rigs. As a result of various delays in building, the parties had made a number of variations to their agreements, both rescheduling and increasing payments substantially. The builder argued that the guarantee agreement expressly excluded the rule in *Holme v Brunskill* and further provided for primary liability on the guarantor's part, although a proviso limited the amount recoverable under the "guarantee" to what would have been recoverable on the basis of a guarantee. In an appeal from a summary judgment finding that it was not arguable that the amendments to the underlying debt were outside the purview of the guarantee, the Court of Appeal looked critically at the authorities comprising the basis of the purview doctrine, including *Triodos*.

The Court of Appeal accepted that the purview doctrine could be seen either as a rule of construction ("do the provisions of the guarantee apply to what has actually happened?") or as a legal doctrine reflecting the equitable concerns of *Holme v Brunskill*: the Court of Appeal clearly did not feel that it could lay down the exact ambit of this "rule" in the context of an appeal from a summary judgment and did not reach a conclusion one way or the other. While it did not exclude the possibility of there being a "rule" imposing a purview doctrine, its status in the modern law was hardly given a resounding recommendation in this particular case although there are too many authorities down the years for it to be disregarded.

As this book is about indemnities, not guarantees, brief mention only will be made of the decision of Registrar Barber in the Bankruptcy Court in *Dowling v Promontoria* [2017] EWHC B25 (Ch) when considering an "all monies" guarantee i.e. a guarantee not limited to one specific agreement but to all present and future liabilities incurred by a debtor to a creditor. The court accepted, on the basis of *Triodos* and *CIMC Raffles*, that a second agreement was not within the "purview" of the all monies guarantee (notwithstanding that neither case concerned an "all monies" guarantee). The decision is not of great authority but has generated a good deal of controversy: whether it would be followed by a higher court with regard to an "all monies" guarantee remains to be seen.

Practice point

The drafting of a parent company guarantee presents considerable problems and contains significant risks to both parties, largely borne of the uncertainty of the application of various legal principles to a guarantee and the extent to which they may be lawfully excluded. The courts will look on the substance of the clause, not what the parties have labelled the provision: just because the agreement describes a party as a primary obligor and not a surety (guarantor) does not necessarily mean that the courts will interpret it as that: this point was accepted at first instance in the *CIMC Raffles* case discussed above, noted with apparent approval by the Court of Appeal,

> *"... the incorporation of a principal debtor clause will not usually suffice in itself to determine the nature of the contract. It will not automatically convert a guarantee into an indemnity."*

This has the curious effect that a clause drafted to be a primary obligation (an indemnity) may nonetheless be construed in context as a guarantee and therefore be subject to the various defences available to guarantors, including the rule in *Holme v Brunskill*. Again, as we have seen, attempts to exclude the effect of the rule in *Holme v Brunskill* are not automatically successful.

In any case, the correct practice was pithily put by Sir Bernard Rix in the Court of Appeal in the same case,

> *"Prudence would in any event have dictated that the guarantor should have been asked for a new guarantee or for a formal indication of consent."*

While wearisome from the point of view of the beneficiary of a guarantee, this is always the safest course of action. For many transactions, minor variations in the underlying debt agreement may well demand the exercise of judgment as to whether further consent from the guarantor should be sought or a new guarantee executed. The reality is, without express wording excluding the effect of the rule in *Holme v Brunskill*, consent will have to be sought in every case where there is a variation to the underlying debt and, in the case of a major variation amounting to a new agreement, the same prudence would demand that a new guarantee should be executed.

As we saw in Chapter One, many agreements as drafted tend to veer wildly between the language of an indemnity, a guarantee and a demand bond, often using the language of all three. It is somewhat like kicking the proverbial can down the street and leaving it to the judge to decide which type of transaction it was if a dispute should ever arise. The difficulty is that, if an obligation is seen as a guarantee, then various equitable defences become available and they may, or may not, be successfully excluded by further express wording in the agreement.

Indemnity against third party claims

This is another very common type of indemnity and a typical example is the nearly ubiquitous IPR indemnity to be found in just about any commercial contract. It has given rise to some confusion among lawyers as to what an indemnity actually is. As we have seen when considering *Firma C-Trade v Newcastle P&I Association (The Fanti) (No 2)* [1991] 2 AC 1[24], the essence of an indemnity, the essence of "holding harmless", is a primary obligation that a defined event will not occur and to be liable in damages as a secondary obligation if it does.

Of course, when drafting e.g. an IPR indemnity, lawyers will put a considerable amount of material around this core idea of an indemnity – what is often referred to as "conduct of indemnity" wording. This might include the indemnified having to give notice of a third party claim to the indemnifier within a given timescale, allowing the indemnifier the sole conduct of the defence of the third party claim and giving assistance to the indemnifier in dealing with that claim. Many lawyers have come to think of this wording as being the indemnity itself, but it is in reality the "wrap" around the indemnity: the indemnity itself as understood in cases like *Firma C-Trade* is the principle of "holding harmless", the undertaking to be liable in damages if the indemnified event (here, a third party IPR claim) occurs.

When drafting these types of indemnity it is important to understand and state explicitly what the indemnity consists of, in particular, when the liability to indemnify arises, which can be important for limitation

---

[24] And more recently in *Minera Las Bambas v Glencore* [2019] EWCA Civ 972 and *Endurance Corporate Capital v Sartex Quilts & Textiles* [2020] EWCA Civ 308

purposes. This is up to the parties to express in their drafting. As Akenhead J put it in *Carillion v Phi Group* [2011] EWHC 1379 (TCC),

> "... *the cause of action for a contractual indemnity arises in effect and practice when the contract in question, properly construed, says that it does.*"

While there are various cases considering this point for limitation purposes, the modern law sees this as an exercise in construing the indemnity provision to establish exactly when liability under it commences. We have already seen a good example of this in *Minera Las Bambas v Glencore* [2019] EWCA Civ 972, where the courts had to construe the beginning of liability under a tax indemnity. Just when was tax "payable" (the word used in the indemnity clause)? The Court of Appeal upheld the judge at first instance in finding that "payable" should be construed as meaning when it was established under Pervian Law by Peruvian courts, not when the Pervuvian tax authorities had earlier assessed the tax: before a judgment of the Peruvian courts, the assessment could not be "coercively enforced" despite an assessment by the tax authorities.

In all of this, the lawyer needs to think carefully about what is meant by offering an indemnity against a "liability" or a "claim", as these terms invite debate about whether what is meant is really a liability established at trial or a claim that would definitely, or would perhaps be likely, to be successful at trial. It should be recalled that the indemnifier, absent any conduct of indemnity wording, is not obliged to do anything about the third party claim unless this can be implied into the wording of the contract. In these types of indemnity, the conduct of indemnity provisions are likely to be of much greater importance as they set out each party's expectations of what it has to do and what it can expect of the other party.

That being so, if a bare indemnity is offered against third party claims then, assuming there is no conduct of indemnity wording and no implied terms to that effect, the indemnified does not have to give notice of the claim to the indemnifier, the indemnifier does not have to lift a finger to assist and, when the indemnified has settled the third party's claim, the indemnifier can then argue that the settlement was unreasonable and that he should not be liable under the indemnity.

We saw with *Ben Shipping v An Bord Bainne (The C Joyce)* [1986] 2 All ER 177 that the court struggled with the idea that simply giving notice to the indemnifier of a third party claim could in some way fix the indemnifier with a duty to defend the indemnified,

> "*[T]he rule contended for would present the charterers with a choice between taking over the defence of a claim which they believed to be nothing to do with them and thereafter (if that belief was falsified) finding themselves bound to indemnify the owners against settlement of a claim even though the claim could be shown to be ill-founded or the settlement unreasonable. The authorities may well support, and I can see virtue in a much more limited principle, but that would not avail the owners here.*"

In other words, the indemnifier is either liable under the indemnity or he is not: the indemnified giving notice cannot of itself fix the indemnifier with a duty to act that he does not have under the strict wording of the indemnity correctly construed.

Indemnity against breach by the indemnifier

These indemnities have become very common in recent years, reflecting the commercial lawyer's increasing use of indemnities generally. A question that should be put to any lawyer drafting these indemnities is, what does the indemnity give that a straight breach of contract claim would not? The answer is very often given that an indemnity claim is much simpler, but even a brief perusal of these pages should give the lie to that proposition. Cases on indemnities have gone in and out of the Court of Appeal on complex points of construction. While this book has presented a version of indemnity "law" largely fashioned from the more modern cases, there are plenty of cases dating back to the early nineteenth century (and beyond) which courts still have to consider from time to time, and which do not necessarily reflect the conclusions reached in the more recent cases.

The very lack of decisive authority on many basic points surrounding indemnities does not seem to deter commercial lawyers from including them. Sometimes, they may have an expectation of what an indemnity will achieve that is not necessarily justifiable when seen against the case-law.

The real problem for an indemnifier is knowing the beginnings and ends of an indemnity against his own breach of contract when compared with a breach of contract claim. With the latter, there are traditionally three concepts which work to limit liability: mitigation, remoteness and causation. Textbooks will provide ample examples of how the law on these areas will be applied. With an indemnity, these principles are (arguably) absent and the court has only the wording of the indemnity to go on, leading to an almost inevitable dispute about the proper construction of the scope and meaning of the indemnity.

It should also be remembered that an indemnity, just like any other provision in a commercial contract, will be interpreted in its context. We saw this in the approach of the Supreme Court in *Wood v Capita Insurance Services* [2017] UKSC 24.

It is of course possible to replicate the common law principles of remoteness, causation and mitigation by inserting appropriate wording into the drafting of the indemnity, at which point one would have to ask whether there was any point in having such an indemnity from the indemnified's point of view. The purpose of the duty to mitigate is to persuade a claimant to behave reasonably so as to minimise any claim for breach of contract. If a party insists therefore on having the benefit of an indemnity without limiting words, it is akin to claiming the right to behave unreasonably. This being so, it is not clear why indemnities given by an indemnifier against his own breach of contract have become so common.

In every case, it will come down to a detailed analysis of the indemnity provision itself. Does it cover breaches by a subcontractor? Does it cover breaches where both the indemnifier and the indemnified are partly responsible? The latter would raise the perhaps dubious status of *Canada Steamship* in the modern law. The courts have somewhat struggled with this, as can be seen by *Total Transport Corp v Arcadia Petroleum (The Eurus)* [1996] 2 Lloyds Rep 408 (QB), where Rix J said, Rix J: a reference to "all consequences" of a breach could be read as including all consequences reasonably contemplated by the parties as a result of the breach

> "... I see force in the argument that, as a matter of construction, a fortiori under a clause where the indemnity is triggered by a breach of contract, the indemnity is subject to the same rules of remoteness as are damages, including the rules under Hadley v. Baxendale. Thus 'all consequences' would mean 'all consequences within the reasonable contemplation of the parties'."

On appeal (*Total Transport Corp v Arcadia Petroleum (The Eurus)* [1998] 1 Lloyds Rep 351 (CA)), Staughton LJ put it more bluntly,

> "... the word 'indemnity' may refer to all loss suffered which is attributable to a specified cause, whether or not it was in the reasonable contemplation of the parties. There is precious little authority to support such a meaning, but I do not doubt that the word is often used in that sense."

Too much cannot be read into this case: the Court of Appeal struggled with the wording, finding that it was not really an indemnity at all and being understandably reluctant to allow the claimants to claim a full indemnity, regardless of the rules on remoteness of loss, for one breach of contract when it could not do so for other breaches.

An example of these issues can be seen in *Bovis Lend Lease v RD Fire Protection* [2003] EWHC 939 (TCC), another complex construction case, this time involving Bovis in seeking to recover under a contractual indemnity in respect of losses it had incurred leading to a settlement with the employer. As the judge (HH Judge Thornton QC) observed after describing the breadth of the drafting,

> "It follows that a claim based on the indemnity is not confined to loss recoverable under the traditional tests for determining

> *recoverable loss resulting from a breach of contract, the causation tests imposed by Hadley v Baxendale and Victoria Laundry v Newman. ..."*

The wording of the indemnity in question ran,

> *"... any act or omission of the Sub-Contractor or his servants or agents which involves [Bovis] in any liability to the Employer under the provision of the Main Contract in so far as they relate and apply to the SubContract ..."*

The loss, for the judge, occurred at the point that liability crystallized – when a claim was brought by the employer leading to a judgment or a reasonable compromise of the claim. Indeed, once there was a settlement, the only liability under the indemnity was the sum payable as a result of the settlement as that was the only loss that had arisen as a result of Bovis' liability to the employer.

This same literalness, perhaps a limitation of the indemnity, can be seen in *Carillion v Phi Group* [2011] EWHC 1379 (TCC) when relating to future liabilities. Carillion was the main contractor on works for M40 Trains, with Phi Group and RWC being subcontractors. The lengthy judgment is about problems encountered with banks of London clay suffering from insufficient support and becoming unstable. Carillion had settled with Phi and now sought recovery from RWC. The indemnity in the relevant contract read,

> *"[RWC] shall indemnify [Carillion] against every liability which [Carillion] may incur to any other person whatsoever and against all claims, losses, demands, proceedings, damages, costs*

and expenses made against or incurred by [Carillion] by reason of any breach by [RWC] of this Consultancy Agreement..."

One question that arose concerning this indemnity is whether it covered the future costs and losses that Carillion would incur: if the court awarded damages in respect of Carillion's costs and expenses, those costs and expenses might never materialise, leaving Carillion overcompensated. Could a declaration of liability under the indemnity be made instead and would it be just to do so?

The court examined the precise wording of the indemnity. The indemnity was against "every liability" that Carillion "may incur to any other person". The existing liability of Carillion to M40 Trains had been established in the trial[25] as *"the design and calculations [were] as careless under all three contracts"* according to the judge. Therefore,

> *"... the entitlement of Carillion to be indemnified against the liability which it has incurred already to M40 Trains is established, even though it has not been established by proceedings or arbitration as between it and M40 Trains or 'realised' in some other way."*

The real question, however, concerned future costs and losses – nothing had been claimed yet against Carillion by M40 Trains, though it had not made any such claim yet and so had not been "incurred". The court concluded that the cause of action based on this part of the indemnity had accordingly not yet arisen. Exercising its discretion, the court

---

[25] Note again that the judge accepted that findings in one trial would not act as *res judicata* in related but separate proceedings: so a finding of liability in this trial would not be binding on the separate proceedings between M40 Trains and Carillion: compare the comments made when discussing *Rust Consulting v PB Limited* above.

declined to grant a declaration as to Carillion's entitlement to indemnity in respect of future losses and instead proceeded to assess the quantum of damages based on the evidence available to it.

The real lesson for those drafting indemnities in respect of the other party's breach of contract is that the result can be unpredictable: the indemnified may well end up with an award of damages greater than would have been awarded for breach of contract (as rules on remoteness, causation and mitigation are either absent or are present in a qualified way). On the other hand, a straight reading of the indemnity may work the other way and achieve the opposite result.

The difference in the level of compensation between an indemnity and a breach of contract claim can be seen in *MAN Nutzfahrzeuge v Freightliner* [2005] EWHC 2347 (Comm). When drafting an indemnity, the parties are creating their own private law, to a large extent divorced from the ordinary and well established legal principles that would apply to a claim for damages following a breach of contract (mitigation, remoteness, causation).

Fortunately, it is not necessary to examine the immensely long judgment: the basic dispute arose from the chronic manipulation of the accounts of ERF, a truck manufacturer, and consequent false claims for repayment of VAT over a number of years. In very brief, MAN succeeded in its claim against Freightliner, the seller of ERF to MAN, for misrepresentation and breach of warranties set out in the Share Purchase Agreement relating to the ERF's accounts and tax (but failed as against E&Y, the auditors).

The SPA contained the following indemnity,

> *"12.1 Indemnification in Favour of MAN*
>
> *... [Freightliner] shall indemnify and hold each of [MAN] harmless of and from any Damages suffered by, imposed or asserted against [MAN] as a result of, in respect of, connected with, or arising out of, under or pursuant to:*
>
> *(a) any failure of [Freightliner] ... to perform or fulfil any of [its] respective covenants under this agreement;*
>
> *(b) any breach or inaccuracy of any representation or warranty given by [Freightliner] ... contained in this Agreement; ..."*

"Damages" was defined to have an extended meaning, namely,

> *"any loss, liability, claim, damage (including incidental and consequential damage) or expense (whether or not involving a third party claim) including legal expenses"*

Clause 12.7 went on to provide,

> *"No Party shall have the right to bring any proceedings against any other Party for a breach of any representation, warranty, covenant or agreement contained in this Agreement, except for a proceeding brought in accordance with the provisions of this Article. This provision is not intended to preclude any proceeding by any Party against any other Party based on fraud or on a cause of action or right, including any statutory right, other than a cause of action in contract or tort for breach of a representation, warranty, covenant or agreement contained in this Agreement."*

The judgment is of extreme length but, for present purposes, one of Freightliner's arguments was that the indemnity formed an exhaustive code for MAN's right to compensation regardless of the basis for the claim (contract, misrepresentation or fraud), and provided for a more limited measure of recovery than that available at common law in respect of the tort of deceit.

The judge (Moore-Bick LJ sitting as a judge of the Commercial Court) went on to hold that the indemnity allowed MAN to recover for misrepresentation as well as breach of warranty. But what recovery did clause 12.1 allow? The answer is not obvious from the parts of the SPA quoted above.

The court accepted that clause 12 was intended by clause 12.7 to be the exclusive remedy – but what claims did clause 12 apply to and what was the measure of indemnity for misrepresentation? The court decided that fraud fell outside the scheme provided by clause 12 but what about misrepresentation? Did the words of clause 12.1 taken together with the definition of "Damages" limit MAN to a contractual level of damages (what was required to make the warranties true) rather than the tortious level of damages for misrepresentation (what was incurred as a result of relying on the misrepresentation)? On one argument, if the tortious level of damages were to be applied, MAN could recover all its trading losses suffered in reliance on the misrepresentation as to ERF's accounts.

For those readers who have persevered so far with the discussion of this one case, it may seem strange that so much debate could be raised by one indemnity clause coupled with a definition of "Damages". After all, one of the purposes of inserting an indemnity with an exclusive remedies provision was to avoid precisely these nice legal arguments.

In the end, the court decided that the wording was clear enough to impose on Freightliner an obligation to indemnify MAN against all the costs and expenses arising out of the inaccuracy of any of the misrepresentations, including losses incurred as a result of taking steps in reliance on their accuracy, but it did not extend to the entire consequences of entering into the agreement insofar as they could not be said to flow from the inaccuracy of the particular representation relied on.

Thus, with regard to the misrepresentation regarding the correct payment of VAT, the indemnity would cover the amounts that ERF was liable to pay by way of arrears of VAT, penalty and expenses incurred in proceedings with the Customs & Excise. The indemnity would not extend to the whole of the loss MAN had suffered in entering into the SPA itself.

Practice point

Be careful of what you wish for: what might seem like a well drafted indemnity covering a multitude of losses, when taken in context, may have less scope than you think or may lead to expensive litigation to resolve. The lesson is that an indemnity is not necessarily a speedy way of resolving disputes but may be just the beginning of a very expensive one.

Indemnity against claims by the indemnifier

At first sight, this seems to be an oxymoron, but such indemnities are commonplace in the construction and engineering fields, where they are often mutual and act as an exclusion of liability in respect of the indemnified subject matter. Very often the aim is to allocate a particular type of loss to each party e.g. to ensure that each party bears the risk of liability for its own employees' death or injury, regardless of which party (or third party) is legally responsible for their accident. We have seen examples of this in discussing the litigation following the Piper Alpha disaster.

We have already discussed a typical case of mutual indemnities when looking at *Transocean Drilling v Providence Resources* [2016] EWCA Civ 372. In reality, there are various ways of looking at this type of drafting:

- It is a mutual release of possible future rights (e.g. *Transocean*)

- It acts as an exclusion of liability (e.g. *Farstad Supply v Enviroco (The Far Service)* [2010] UKSC 18)

- It has the same effect as a promise not to commence proceedings (e.g. *Deepak Fertilisers and Petrochemicals v ICI* [1999] 1 Lloyds Rep 387 (CA))

There are probably other ways of looking at it. Perhaps the only point that needs to be made in this context is that mutual must mean exactly that: problems may occur if the mutual indemnities are not in exactly the same form. An example of this can be seen in *Campbell v Conoco* [2002] EWCA Civ 704, which was considered briefly in Chapter Four, although the court overlooked the slight differences between the two indemnities in favour of a purposeful, contextual construction. The words that were different were,

"... all claims arising in respect of any injury ..."

Did this wording capture liability under an indemnity in a back to back contract? Seen on its own, it might suggest just a direct liability for personal injuries. However, as already stated, the Court of Appeal took a pragmatic view and applied what was obviously the intention of the parties: Salamis was liable to indemnify Amec, which was bound to indemnify Conoco for the injuries sustained by Campbell.

MORE BOOKS BY
LAW BRIEF PUBLISHING

A selection of our other titles available now:-

'Covid-19, Homeworking and the Law – The Essential Guide to Employment and GDPR Issues' by Forbes Solicitors
'Covid-19, Force Majeure and Frustration of Contracts – The Essential Guide' by Keith Markham
'Covid-19 and Criminal Law – The Essential Guide' by Ramya Nagesh
'Covid-19 and Family Law in England and Wales – The Essential Guide' by Safda Mahmood
'Covid-19 and the Implications for Planning Law – The Essential Guide' by Bob Mc Geady & Meyric Lewis
'Covid-19, Residential Property, Equity Release and Enfranchisement – The Essential Guide' by Paul Sams and Louise Uphill
'Covid-19, Brexit and the Law of Commercial Leases – The Essential Guide' by Mark Shelton
'Covid-19 and the Law Relating to Food in the UK and Republic of Ireland – The Essential Guide' by Ian Thomas
'A Practical Guide to the General Data Protection Regulation (GDPR) – 2nd Edition' by Keith Markham
'Ellis on Credit Hire – Sixth Edition' by Aidan Ellis & Tim Kevan
'A Practical Guide to Working with Litigants in Person and McKenzie Friends in Family Cases' by Stuart Barlow

'A Practical Guide to Compliance for Personal Injury Firms Working With Claims Management Companies' by Paul Bennett
'A Practical Guide to the Landlord and Tenant Act 1954: Commercial Tenancies' by Richard Hayes & David Sawtell
'A Practical Guide to Dog Law for Owners and Others' by Andrea Pitt
'RTA Allegations of Fraud in a Post-Jackson Era: The Handbook – 2nd Edition' by Andrew Mckie
'RTA Personal Injury Claims: A Practical Guide Post-Jackson' by Andrew Mckie
'On Experts: CPR35 for Lawyers and Experts' by David Boyle
'An Introduction to Personal Injury Law' by David Boyle
'A Practical Guide to Chronic Pain Claims' by Pankaj Madan
'A Practical Guide to Claims Arising from Fatal Accidents' by James Patience
'A Practical Guide to Subtle Brain Injury Claims' by Pankaj Madan

These books and more are available to order online direct from the publisher at www.lawbriefpublishing.com, where you can also read free sample chapters. For any queries, contact us on 0844 587 2383 or mail@lawbriefpublishing.com.

Our books are also usually in stock at www.amazon.co.uk with free next day delivery for Prime members, and at good legal bookshops such as Wildy & Sons.

We are regularly launching new books in our series of practical day-to-day practitioners' guides. Visit our website and join our free newsletter to be kept informed and to receive special offers, free chapters, etc.

You can also follow us on Twitter at www.twitter.com/lawbriefpub.

Printed in Great Britain
by Amazon